Morgan Freeman & Friends

Morgan Freeman & Friends

CARIBBEAN COOKING FOR A CAUSE

WENDY WILKINSON *and* DONNA LEE

Introduction by MORGAN FREEMAN

RODALE

Rodale Inc. makes every effort to use acid-free ⊗, recycled paper ♻.

Interior photo credits appear on page 249.

Map illustration, page xii, by Sylvia Hofflund

Book design by Patricia Field

Library of Congress Cataloging-in-Publication Data

Wilkinson, Wendy (Wendy Ann), date
    Morgan Freeman & friends : Caribbean cooking for a cause / Wendy Wilkinson and Donna Lee ; introduction by Morgan Freeman.
        p.   cm.
    Includes index.
    ISBN-13 978–1–59486–424–7   hardcover
    ISBN-10 1–59486–424–1   hardcover
    1. Cookery, Caribbean.   I. Lee, Donna Marie.   II. Freeman, Morgan.   III. Title.
TX716.A1W55   2006
641.5′9729—dc22   2006023817

Distributed to the trade by Holtzbrinck Publishers

2   4   6   8   10   9   7   5   3   1   hardcover

To Champie Evans and the people of the Caribbean Islands, with our love;
and to Linda, who embodied the vibrancy of Caribbean cooking,
Southern soul food, and so much more.

—Morgan and Donna

This book is dedicated to my husband, Dennis,
who found our Abaco Island retreat and fostered my love
of everything Caribbean; and to my daughter, Alexandra,
and mother, Beverly, who share my island adventures.

—Wendy

And a special dedication to those on the magical island of Grenada
who both sadly succumbed, but more importantly survived Ivan the Terrible
and are well underway to rebuilding their lives and island.

ACKNOWLEDGMENTS

We are so pleased to help benefit the Grenada Relief Fund, an organization founded with Morgan, to help provide aid to the capable island of Grenada.

We thank the many people and organizations that provided their time, guidance, and expertise and helped us to turn this book idea into a reality. They include: the Ariel Sands Resort, Lee Brillstein, Anya Bierzynski and the Bierzynski family, Alan Burry, Allison Diamond, Dixie Dunbar, Alan Eichorn, Kelly Dylan Fiore, Victoria Fredrick, the magnificent Mehdi Eftekari, Sarah Cairns, Lena Elfmont and the Four Seasons Hotel in Beverly Hills, Tara MacIntyre and Martin Sinclair and the Four Seasons in Nevis, Clint Highman, Talin Kalfayan, Kathleen Lobb, Ray McKigney, Melody Kornblatt, Mike Langresse, Laureus Sport for Good, Michele P. Lee, Debbi O'Loughlin, Jane Meffmore, Natalie Miller, Julie Nathanson, Rosalind Napoli and the Loews' Hotel in Santa Monica, Sooki Raphael, Radha Arora and the Regent, Beverly Wilshire, Nikki Parker, Krista Renjard, Pamela C. Richards, Anna Banana Roth, Leigh Greenberg Secker, Michael Singer, Ken Sunshine and Company, Claudio Vigilante, Marvin Wamble and Family, D. J. Walton, Kim Wang and Shutters at the Beach, Jon Whitticom, and Williams & Connolly, LLP.

A particular debt of gratitude is owed to Jeff Berman, and also Julia Chester and Mike Clarke of Sidley Austin, LLP, on behalf of the Grenada Relief Fund.

We would also like to express our appreciation to the gifted professionals—especially Harley Marion and Catherine Robinson—at Shewmaker's Camera in Colorado Springs, Colorado, for their time, talent, and expertise in editing and color-correcting the hundreds of images.

Finally, huge thanks and gratitude to our wonderful agent, Stephanie Tade, and our three editors at Rodale, Margot Schupf, Miriam Backes, and Jennifer DeFilippi, as well as Kimberly Tweed, Patricia Field, Hope Clarke, Keith Biery, and Meghan Phillips.

CONTENTS

INTRODUCTION

BY MORGAN FREEMAN

Love at first sight does exist. The first time I set eyes on a sailboat was in 1961. Graceful as a swan, it was gliding sensuously on San Francisco Bay, and I was smitten. Six years later, while working at the Stowe Playhouse in Stowe, Vermont, I sailed for the first time—on a reservoir in an 18-foot (5.49-meter) Lightning-class centerboard boat. Then I was not only smitten, I was hooked for life. Ever since those halcyon days, sailing has been more than a pastime for me—it has been my refuge and my passion.

I bought my first boat, a Holland-built Holiday 28, in Huntington Bay, Long Island, in 1971. By then, I was beginning to make good in New York theater. I was standby for Cleavon Little, who was starring in *Purlie,* and I had landed a plum television role on *The Electric Company.* I developed my skills as a sailor plying the waters off the coasts of Massachusetts and Maine. Those rough-and-tumble waters will develop a person's sea legs like no others can. And I was a young man with a taste for the challenge. What with the nor'easters, the fog, and the swift current, my sailing skills were honed to a pretty fine edge.

For 16 years, I sailed out of Eastchester Bay, many times in the company of my dear friends Mel and Jane Boudrot, pretty much covering the waters and anchorages of Long Island Sound, Block Island, the Elizabeth Islands, Cape Cod, the coast of Maine, and up to Yarmouth, Nova Scotia. I am grateful now for the technical expertise I gained in the waters of the Northeast Coast. Sailing along these rocky coasts, sometimes in a blind fog, readied me for the extraordinary and challenging beauty I was to discover in the Caribbean.

I first sailed south in 1979, going to Bermuda on a 30-foot (9.14-meter) Alberg-designed sloop. The crew included my wife, Myrna; my youngest daughter, Morgana; and our cat, Zipper. It took 9 days to get there, and we stayed for 6 weeks, anchored in the shelter of White's Island in Hamilton Harbor. On the way back to New York in October, we hit our survival storm. Two hundred fifty

miles due east of Newport News, Virginia, we ran into the worst weather I have ever experienced—sustained 50-knot winds and seas that appeared mountainous to me in my little sloop. Luckily, Morgana had already gone back to school, so it was just me, a deathly seasick Myrna, and Zipper on board. It is an experience that I will never, ever forget. It's like an exclamation point in my life.

Our first sail all the way to the Caribbean was in late summer of 1989. This time, I was with Myrna; one of our grandchildren, E'dena; and two friends, Billy Toles and Harry Smith, as crew. Six days out of Bermuda on our Shannon 38, *Sojourner,* we raised the light on Sombrero Rock, north of St. Martin, around 9:00 p.m. Two years later, we sailed across to the British Virgin Islands (BVI), and I knew I had found my way to paradise. The beauty of these islands is incomparable.

In 1993, I asked Harry to sail with me to the Spice Islands just for a look-see, and that's when I met my first Grenadian. His name is Champie, and he is still my friend today. Harry and I and his then-wife, Linda, gunkholed up the Grenadines as far as St. Lucia before heading back across the sea to the BVI.

Five years later, and with a new Shannon 43, Harry, Billy, and I set sail for Trinidad and then to the island of Grenada, the anchor of the spectacular Grenadines and a true sailor's delight. The island has a fascinating history, which you will learn more about in this book, and its people are kind, generous, and full of fun.

The Grenadines are now a second home to me. I feel protective of them. I want their pristine beauty, their mystery, and their "serenity in motion" to last forever. When Hurricane Ivan hit Grenada in 2004, I was beyond despair. The storm brought devastation to my friends, their homes,

and their livelihoods. You never know just what to do in situations like that, but something has to be done.

The inspiration for this book came from two sources: my desire to help the people of Grenada and my cherished sister-in-law, cowriter Donna Lee. When Champie called me after the hurricane, I called Donna, and the idea was born. We thought maybe I could share Grenada and her island neighbors with people who hadn't experienced them firsthand. We could point out how important it is to restore, protect, and preserve this part of the world.

My hope for this book is not only that it raises boatloads of money for the Grenada Relief Fund and thereby helps my island friends, but also that you who are reading it will experience in some small way the joy that I have experienced in these islands. So we've organized the book as I would plan a sailing trip—making time for friends, for exquisite food, and for the beauty and uniqueness of the many islands we visit.

Enjoy.

BERMUDA

Michael Douglas

BERMUDA BRED

A star both behind and in front of the camera, Michael Douglas got his start working on the crews of the films produced by his father, Kirk. In the 1970s, Michael's executive-producing debut, *One Flew Over the Cuckoo's Nest,* earned five Oscars, including one for Best Picture. *The China Syndrome, Made in America,* and *The Rainmaker,* among others, soon followed. As an actor, he is acclaimed for the manically driven characters he's played in psychological thrillers such as *The Game, Wall Street, Disclosure, A Perfect Murder,* and *War of the Roses.*

What many people don't know, however, is that he is also—and earnestly—Bermudian. The grandson of an attorney general of Bermuda, Michael spent many happy times there with his mother, actress Diana Dill, and his maternal relatives. He has fond memories of combing the landscape and beaches, and he cherishes the island's quintessential tranquility and gentle people. Now, he and his wife, actress Catherine Zeta-Jones, have made the island their primary residence, perhaps with the hope that their two children will experience similar serenity. And with a beloved "town crier" who shouts "I love you" to the population daily, life there is indeed very, very good.

At the bottom of a slope of verdant pasture dotted with coral bungalows is a blue-green lagoon. It's surprising to see what appears to be a child out in the opalescent water, 40 feet (12.19 meters) from shore, playing with a mirror. When you look more closely, it becomes clear that the child is actually a gleaming statue. It is Ariel, the sprite of Shakespeare's *The Tempest,* frolicking in the waters along Ariel Sands, the quaint resort that bears his name.

While the Douglas manse itself is nearby, Ariel Sands is home, at least figuratively, for Michael Douglas. "The Dills—my mother's family—owned this land," explains Michael. "Ariel Sands was a 14-acre (0.06 square kilometer) parcel of pastureland. I got together with a couple of my relatives—I've got about 40 family members living on the island—and we came up with this."

"This" includes the award-winning Aqua Restaurant. According to the restaurant's owner and manager, Claudio Vigilante, "Michael is very involved, as is his family, in this resort. They have a genuine love for their fellow Bermudians. People always expect a top-shelf experience from a family-owned business, and the expectations for quality go up—because it's Michael.

"Each year, there is better and better dialogue with the local fishermen. The beauty of being a restaurant owner on an island is that the locals will work with you to develop product. And our locals are very sophisticated and smart—just like the clientele," says Claudio. "Many people visit here, and they all bring something of their culture and ideas. That creates a big canvas and helps us to produce sophisticated food."

Aqua is known for its Asian-fusion cuisine, focusing on fresh fish and always offering at least one fresh fish special. But because Bermuda is an international port that has benefited from the continuous influence of many cultures, the restaurant's management doesn't restrict itself to one particular type of food and is willing to try dishes with French leanings, as well as Italian and Indian. Aqua thrives on invention, and its only constant is creativity. In fact, the restaurant has won culinary awards that cite these very qualities.

Michael has his own ideas about the source of Bermudian creativity. "I think because we're out here by ourselves, about 600 miles (966 kilometers) off the coast of North Carolina—there's nothing out here—that people are used to living by their wits. We figure things out in Bermuda."

Such inventiveness works not only for the hospitality industry but also for survival in times of crisis. "Almost every building here is made from Bermuda stone. That helps a lot, but luckily we've

had only three direct hits from hurricanes in the past century. Fabian, a few years ago, was one of them," he says. "When I saw what happened to Grenada, my heart went out to them because we know from our own experience."

"We were working when Fabian was due to reach Bermuda," adds Claudio. "We had a wedding party that day—they were supposed to get married on the beach. You get false alarms—that's the nature of these storms; they are unpredictable. But the staff generally knows at some point that we're really going to get hit. There is pressure in the air. Two hours before the storm, we looked out at the ocean, and it literally looked like a mountain of water was coming toward us. We locked and bolted all that we could the traditional way, battening down all of the beach and bar equipment, the food and liquor—anything that could be destroyed by water. The storm raged. It just went on all day, all night. Come daylight—6:30—the destruction of the island was revealed.

"The roads were covered with debris. Palm trees were stacked like cards, one on top of the other," he recalls. "When we got to the hotel, the umbrellas were everywhere; great trees that had stood for 60 or 70 years were down. The roofs of the cottages were pulled off, but the main structure of the hotel stood firm. Michael sent planefuls of emergency supplies down to us and to other stations on the island. Four days later, we reopened the restaurant."

Solid native stonework and the quick clearing of trees aside, it isn't a surprise that Bermuda weathers storms well. Visitors to the island often comment on the characteristic Bermudian composure. "The fact is, the wealth of the island—the reinsurance companies and the offshore financing companies—make for a strong infrastructure," says Michael. "But this is also an island of faith. There have got to be more churches per capita in Bermuda than on any other island. And that makes for a strong core. I find it the most racially comfortable place—it's about 60/40 black, and we just get along. The different races that mix here—Portuguese, West Indian, Dutch—we're strong. And we pull together."

One evening, at a reception Michael and Catherine hosted for the Grenada Relief Fund, a friend presented him with a statuette of a brown figure with arms outstretched. "Oh, my goodness. It's Johnny Barnes!" he cried out in delight. The Bermudians in the room chuckled and smiled knowingly.

"Johnny Barnes," Michael explains, "is the kindest person in the world, I think. Almost every morning, he stands at the entrance of Crow Lane roundabout in the town of Hamilton and just waves and blows kisses. He literally shouts 'I love you' to the motorists and pedestrians over and over again. It's really something," he says, his eyes misting slightly. It's clear that, in his heart, Michael Douglas shouts these words to Bermuda every day, too.

AQUA RESTAURANT,
ARIEL SANDS RESORT

Devonshire, Bermuda

John Wason, Executive Chef

No one on the island was surprised when the Aqua Restaurant at the tranquil Ariel Sands Resort received the *Bermudian* magazine's Bermuda Gold awards for Most Imaginative Menu and Best Chef in 2004. Chef John Wason and the restaurant's owner/manager, Claudio Vigilante, are well known for nurturing creativity in their kitchen.

John was raised in Barbados by a stern mother and a strict father who wanted him to study auto body repair. But John wanted only to cook. When it came down to a standoff with his father, he took the age-old option and went to sea, cooking on big ships and oil rigs with the merchant marines. It was a hard life, but traveling to places like Trinidad, Cuba, Spain, and Suriname gave him the foundation he craved—an encyclopedic knowledge of international ingredients, culinary traditions, and cooking techniques. A subsequent stint on a cruise ship gave him the opportunity to refine his style.

Eventually, John settled in Bermuda, working as a sous chef at a small restaurant in St. George. Then, 7 years ago, he joined the Ariel Sands family, where he and a former Ariel Sands chef named Troy were encouraged to let their creativity flow. Ever since, there have been culinary awards and a filled-to-capacity dining room every weekend night.

"Aqua specializes in new Asian and Continental cuisine but with a Bermudian flair," John says. "The star item on the menu is the Lobster Kabuki. It's Japanese, with a batter similar to that of tempura. It's served with a mango and green papaya salad. When it's lobster season—from September to the end of March—you have to take full advantage.

"Our bouillabaisse is basically Mediterranean, but we put a little spiced black rum into it. That's the kick. It goes well with a Dark 'n Stormy." This strictly Bermudian drink is composed of one part Bermuda black rum and two parts Bermuda ginger beer.

"Next time he comes, I'll make a Dark 'n Stormy for Mr. Douglas," says John. "He loves Bermu-

dian fish, so I'll also make him the rockfish with casaba melon—he's been very impressed with this dish in the past."

Still passionately committed to creative cooking, John says, "I go home at night, get out a piece of paper, and write"—like a songwriter. "Ideas for new recipes fly into my head these days."

The chef's personal motto? "I feel in my heart that if you know that you can be better, be better." This belief is evident not only in his cooking but also in his heartfelt link to the Caribbean and US Gulf territories that have been so affected by hurricanes and storms in recent years. "Bermuda is linked to the Caribbean—the dockyards were built by the West Indian regiments during the First and Second World Wars. A lot of these people never went home. We feel a very strong connection to the Caribbean islands. In my heart, I strongly believe that we are one people. The same hurricane that destroyed Grenada also took a piece of Barbados—my home. We must look out for each other."

Bermuda Bouillabaisse

AQUA RESTAURANT, ARIEL SANDS RESORT, CHEF JOHN WASON

This flavorful classic, brimming with fresh seafood, is guaranteed to make you feel swept away. A splash of sherry pepper and dark rum add a distinctive island touch.

Makes 4 to 6 servings

¼ CUP (60 ML) VEGETABLE OIL

1 SMALL ONION, THINLY SLICED

2 CLOVES GARLIC, CHOPPED

1 BAY LEAF

2 SPRIGS FRESH THYME

2 PINCHES CURRY POWDER

6 TABLESPOONS (90 ML) TOMATO PASTE

2 TOMATOES, DICED

2 CUPS (480 ML) V8 VEGETABLE JUICE

2 CUPS (480 ML) FISH STOCK OR CHICKEN BROTH

2 POUNDS (1 KG) MUSSELS, SCRUBBED

1 POUND (454 G) COMBINED ROCKFISH AND WAHOO, SKINNED IF NECESSARY AND CUT INTO BITE-SIZE PIECES

1 POUND (454 G) LOBSTER MEAT CUT INTO BITE-SIZE PIECES

1 POUND (454 G) SHRIMP, PEELED AND DEVEINED, TAILS REMOVED

1 TEASPOON (5 ML) SALT

½ TEASPOON (2.5 ML) FRESHLY GROUND BLACK PEPPER

1½ TEASPOONS (7.5 ML) FRESH LEMON JUICE

1 CUP (240 ML) DICED BELL PEPPER

1 POUND (454 G) CABOCHA OR BUTTERNUT SQUASH, PEELED AND DICED

1 POUND (454 G) FRESH SPINACH, STEMMED AND WASHED

¼ CUP (60 ML) COMBINED SHERRY PEPPER (SEE RESOURCES, PAGE 246) AND DARK RUM

GARLIC CROSTINI (SEE NOTE)

Heat 2 tablespoons (30 ml) of the oil in a large pot over medium heat. Add the onion, garlic, and bay leaf and sauté for 8 to 10 minutes, or until soft. Add the thyme, curry powder, tomato paste, tomatoes, V8, and stock and simmer for 5 to 7 minutes. Season to taste with salt and pepper and set aside.

Carefully pick over the mussels and discard any that have opened (tap gently on the shells to see if they'll close). Sprinkle the fish, lobster, and shrimp with the salt, pepper, and lemon juice. Heat the remaining oil in a large skillet over medium-high heat. Add the fish, shrimp, peppers, and squash and cook, stirring, for 2 minutes. Add the lobster, spinach, and mussels, then stir in the reserved soup mixture, cover, and simmer for 5 to 7 minutes, until the mussels open and the seafood is opaque. Remove from the heat and discard any unopened mussels. Remove the bay leaf. Stir in the sherry pepper and rum. Serve garnished with the crostini.

NOTE: *To make garlic crostini, preheat the oven to 350°F (180°C). Cut a garlic clove in half and rub it over thin slices of French bread. Drizzle with olive oil and bake for 15 to 20 minutes, or until crisp. You can make the crostini up to 24 hours ahead; store covered at room temperature until ready to serve.*

Chicken Roti

AQUA RESTAURANT, ARIEL SANDS RESORT, CHEF JOHN WASON

This delicious curry is extremely versatile. Substitute equal amounts of lamb, beef, firm white fish, or vegetables if you prefer. Any of these options are irresistible wrapped in a fresh, tortilla-like roti wrapper.

Makes 8 servings

½ CUP (120 ML) VEGETABLE OIL + ADDITIONAL TO BRUSH ROTIS

1½ LARGE ONIONS, VERY FINELY CHOPPED (ABOUT 1½ CUPS [360 ML])

4 CLOVES GARLIC, CHOPPED

1 TEASPOON (5 ML) FINELY CHOPPED FRESH GINGER

2 TEASPOONS (10 ML) GROUND CORIANDER

1 TEASPOON (5 ML) GROUND TURMERIC

1 TEASPOON (5 ML) GROUND CUMIN

1 TEASPOON (5 ML) GARAM MASALA

½ TEASPOON (2.5 ML) CAYENNE PEPPER

2½ CUPS (600 ML) WATER

4 MEDIUM TOMATOES, CHOPPED

SALT AND FRESHLY GROUND BLACK PEPPER

2 POUNDS (1 KG) BONELESS CHICKEN, CUT INTO BITE-SIZE PIECES

¾ POUND (340 G) POTATOES, PEELED AND DICED (ABOUT 1¾ CUPS [420 ML])

8 ROTI WRAPPERS (SEE RESOURCES, PAGE 246)

CHOPPED FRESH CILANTRO

Heat the oil in a heavy skillet over medium heat. Add the onions and cook for 15 to 20 minutes, or until deep brown. Add the garlic and ginger and cook for 1 minute, or until fragrant. Add the coriander and stir for 1 minute to blend. Reduce the heat to low, add the turmeric, cumin, garam masala, and cayenne and cook for 10 minutes. Increase the heat to medium-high, add 1 cup (240 ml) of the water, and cook for 10 minutes, or until the sauce begins to thicken. Add the tomatoes, stir well, and cook for 5 minutes. Season to taste with the salt and pepper.

Add the chicken and cook, stirring, for 3 minutes, or until coated with the onion mixture. Add the potatoes and the remaining 1½ cups (360 ml) water. Cook for about 10 minutes, or until the chicken is no longer pink inside and the potatoes are tender.

To heat the wrappers, heat a griddle or large skillet over high heat. Working one at a time, brush both sides of the wrappers lightly with vegetable oil and cook for about 2 minutes on each side. As each wrapper is done, transfer to greaseproof paper.

To assemble the dish, spoon equal portions of curry onto the wrappers, garnish with the cilantro, and fold over. Serve hot.

Island Coconut Cheesecake

AQUA RESTAURANT, ARIEL SANDS RESORT, CHEF JOHN WASON

Makes 12 servings

CRUST

1 CUP (240 ML) GRAHAM CRACKER CRUMBS

¼ CUP (60 ML) TOASTED SHREDDED COCONUT

1 EGG WHITE

¼ CUP (60 ML) BUTTER, MELTED

¼ CUP (60 ML) SUGAR

FILLING

¾ CUP (180 ML) SUGAR

2 TABLESPOONS (30 ML) CORNSTARCH

GRATED ZEST OF 1 LEMON

3 PACKAGES (8 OUNCES [227 G] EACH) CREAM CHEESE, AT ROOM TEMPERATURE

3 EGGS

½ CUP (120 ML) COCONUT MILK

1 TABLESPOON (15 ML) COCONUT EXTRACT

Preheat the oven to 350°F (180°C). Coat a 9" (23 cm) springform pan with cooking spray.

TO MAKE THE CRUST: In a large bowl, combine the graham cracker crumbs, coconut, egg white, butter, and sugar, stirring with a fork until well blended. With the palm of your hand, press the mixture into the bottom of the prepared pan and set aside.

TO MAKE THE FILLING: In another large bowl, using an electric mixer on low speed, combine the sugar, cornstarch, and lemon zest and mix for 1 minute. Set the mixer on medium speed and add the cream cheese in batches, mixing after each addition until smooth, about 1 minute. Add the eggs one at a time, and then mix for 3 minutes. Scrape down the sides of the bowl and set the mixer on low speed. Slowly add the coconut milk and extract and mix for 3 minutes, or until smooth. Pour the batter into the prepared pan and set inside a larger pan. Place in the oven and fill the larger pan with enough water to come ¾" (2 cm) up the sides of the springform pan. Bake for 1 hour to 1 hour and 15 minutes, or until golden brown and set in the middle (it should jiggle slightly when the pan is gently shaken). Let cool to room temperature, then refrigerate for at least 1 hour before serving.

CUBA

Daisy Fuentes

A Taste of Cuba in Miami

Television host extraordinaire Daisy Fuentes was barely in her twenties when she became the first crossover VJ, appearing on both Spanish-language and English MTV. She was the first Latina Revlon model and international cover girl, and she was host of the Miss Universe Pageant 3 years in a row. Always true to her Latina roots, she hosted the 2004 Latin Grammy Awards preshow, for which she was honored with an Emmy for Outstanding Achievement in Hosting. As funny as she is beautiful, Daisy also hosted *America's Funniest Home Videos* for 3 years and has been a guest star in various hit comedy series.

In March 2004, she launched her own line of women's sportswear, DF Daisy Fuentes Moda, which is sold exclusively at KOHL's department stores nationwide.

Over the past several years, Daisy has developed a deep appreciation for the Cuban/Spanish–influenced cooking that is so strongly rooted in her family's culture and home life. One of her favorite pastimes in Miami, she says, is to go shopping with her mother for all the wonderful Cuban spices and foods so the two of them can spend the afternoon cooking together.

Daisy says that every time she goes to Miami, she feels as if she is having an island experience. Although her family moved to Spain when she was just 3 years old, she has memories of her native Cuba and of wonderful family dinners, which she still enjoys in Miami, where there is a huge Cuban community. In fact, she can remember her grandparents saying that there was "something in the air" in South Florida that reminded them of home.

"My grandfather used to mark special family gatherings by roasting a pig on our farm in Cuba, and years later, he prepared the same outdoor feast in Miami. He grew plants, fruits, and vegetables along one whole side of the house, literally bringing a part of his farm across the Caribbean to Miami," she remembers. "It made him feel as if he was in the fields of Cuba bringing home produce for the dinner table.

"Even now, whenever I go home, my family starts planning dinner at the breakfast table. Most of our day is spent organizing the meals. Who is going to cook—me, my mom, or Dad—and what will we prepare?"

Daisy's family blends Cuban and Spanish traditions and cultures, and this intermingling is very evident in the kitchen, where even the most traditional Cuban dishes include a Spanish influence.

"The recipes are handed down from generation to generation. The dishes my grandmother cooks now are the ones she was cooking when I was 5, and she's still cooking them exactly the same way today," explains Daisy. "When I prepare some of the dishes my grandmother cooks, I try to never lose the authenticity, even though I do alter them a bit because I have to watch my weight."

Arroz Con Pollo, which is one of Daisy's favorite traditional dishes, is prepared in her family "almost on autopilot," she says. "I remember trying to get a recipe from my mother and grandmother and finding out there is no such thing. I love that about my family's meal preparation. My grandmother will say, 'Take a pinch of this and that,' and I'll ask, 'But what is a pinch?' I try to explain that not everybody knows this 'universal kitchen pinch,' but that's what makes the food so wonderful and authentic."

In a Latin kitchen, anything goes, according to Daisy, and if they don't have the exact items called for in a dish, the cooks in her family frequently start pulling things out of the pantry and refrigerator at random, adding a little bit of "whatever," depending upon what happens to be on hand. When they're done, they make up a name for their creation.

Sitting together around the table, especially during the holidays, is an important tradition in her family. "I come from a working-class background, and when I was growing up, we always tried to have dinner with as many family members as we could. Everything was discussed at the table, and we would all get involved with what was going on in the family as well as outside of it."

When she was a little girl, Daisy was a very fussy eater, and her grandparents often had to be very creative just to get her to eat. "I remember thinking I was a pig, so my grandfather would carry me out to the barn and let me eat with the pigs while he was feeding them from his hip pocket. I loved eating with the animals, but someone put a stop to it somewhere along the way."

Luckily, Daisy's culinary tastes have matured since those days, and she has also come to appreciate a healthier approach to food. "When I was growing up, my mom would prepare great home-cooked meals, but often I didn't really appreciate them and preferred to go out for a pizza. It wasn't until I moved out of the house that I realized how wonderful these culinary traditions really were and wanted to learn more about them."

Daisy and her great-grandmother

Four generations of Fuentes women

Her mother, a breast cancer survivor, has kept the essence of the original family recipes but now adds a lot more vegetables and greens. She doesn't prepare as many fried foods, and salads now play a much bigger part in her meals.

"Picadillo is one of my favorite recipes," Daisy says. "When I make it traditionally, it reminds me of home, but if I'm working and watching what I eat, I make it with fresh turkey or chicken instead of pork and beef."

Another favorite is Sofrito—chopped onions, fresh garlic, peppers, red saffron spice, and olive oil. This dish is the nucleus of most Cuban main dishes. When you start any dish with a sofrito, it will have a bit of Cuban flavor and, according to Daisy, "Once it starts cooking, the smell around the house is amazing. It means it's dinnertime."

Picadillo

FROM THE KITCHEN OF DAISY'S GRANDMOTHER

Makes 4 servings

3 TABLESPOONS (45 ML) OLIVE OIL

1 LARGE SPANISH ONION, CHOPPED

2 GREEN BELL PEPPERS, CORED, SEEDED, AND
   CHOPPED

4 CLOVES GARLIC, MINCED

1 CHILE PEPPER, MINCED (SEE NOTE)

1 POUND (454 G) LEAN GROUND BEEF

1 CUP (240 ML) TOMATO SAUCE

SALT AND FRESHLY GROUND BLACK PEPPER

¼ CUP (60 ML) DRY RED WINE

½ CUP (120 ML) SLICED PITTED GREEN OLIVES

¼ CUP (60 ML) RAISINS (OPTIONAL)

WHITE RICE OR MASHED POTATOES (OPTIONAL)

Heat the oil in a large skillet over medium-high heat. Add the onion, bell peppers, garlic, and chile pepper and sauté until tender but not browned. Add the beef and cook, stirring occasionally and breaking up the meat with the back of a spoon, until browned. Stir in the tomato sauce and season to taste with the salt and black pepper. Cover, reduce the heat to medium-low, and simmer for about 15 minutes. Uncover and stir in the wine, olives, and raisins (if using). Cook for about 15 minutes, or until the liquid is reduced by one-third. Serve with rice or mashed potatoes, if desired.

NOTE: *Wear plastic gloves when handling chile peppers, and wash your hands thoroughly with soap and water before touching sensitive parts of your body, especially your face. To reduce the heat in the finished dish, use only the sides of the pepper (discard seeds and core).*

Arroz Con Pollo

FROM THE KITCHEN OF DAISY'S GRANDMOTHER

Makes 6 servings

1 LARGE CHICKEN (4–5 POUNDS [1.8–2.2 KG])

¾ TEASPOON (3.7 ML) SALT

¼ TEASPOON (1.2 ML) FRESHLY GROUND BLACK
    PEPPER

3 TABLESPOONS (45 ML) OLIVE OIL

1 LARGE SPANISH ONION, SLICED

1 GREEN BELL PEPPER, SLICED

3 CLOVES GARLIC, MINCED

2 CUPS (480 ML) WHITE RICE

½ CUP (120 ML) DRY WHITE WINE

4 CUPS (1 L) CHICKEN STOCK

¼ TEASPOON (1.2 ML) SAFFRON OR GOYA
    POWDERED SPANISH SEASONING MIX

2 CUPS (480 ML) PEAS

Preheat the oven to 350°F (180°C).

Cut up the chicken, separating the legs from the thighs, removing the wings from the breast, and cutting the breast into 4 pieces (10 pieces in all; remove the skin if you prefer a leaner dish). Season with ½ teaspoon (2.5 ml) of the salt and the black pepper.

Heat the oil in a large Dutch oven over medium heat. Add the chicken and cook, turning frequently, until well browned on all sides. Transfer to a plate and set aside. Add the onion, bell pepper, garlic, and rice to the pan and cook, stirring frequently, until the vegetables are tender (if the rice sticks, add a bit more oil).

Arrange the chicken on top of the vegetables, then add the wine and stock. Add the saffron and remaining salt and bring to a boil, stirring occasionally. Remove from the heat and cover with foil. Bake for about 20 minutes, or until the rice is tender. Uncover and stir in the peas. Return to the oven and bake for an additional 5 minutes.

BAHAMAS

THE CLUBHOUSE RESTAURANT,
THE ABACO CLUB ON WINDING BAY

Abaco, Bahamas

Chef Samuel Favella

The striking Clubhouse Restaurant at the Abaco Club on Winding Bay does feel a lot like a country club. Tall beams rise to a circular roof, but the sides are left open to let in the sights and sounds of the rambling 520-acre (2.1-squared kilometers) private seaside resort.

Chef Samuel Favella began his Bahamian cooking career 9 years ago as executive banquet chef at the Atlantis resort in Nassau. From there, he went first to cook on a private island and then at Abaco's Green Turtle Cay before landing at the Oak Dock Restaurant at the Marina. Finally, he accepted an offer he couldn't refuse from owner Peter de Savary, and he has been executive chef at the Clubhouse Restaurant since the membership resort was started in 2004.

It is a culinary goal for the Clubhouse to feature as many local specialties as possible, and one of the restaurant's most popular dishes is the island suckling pig. "I roast the pig and serve it with my own homemade mango chutney salsa," says Samuel. "I also add fever grass, which is most commonly used in Thai cooking and has a nutty lemon flavor similar to that of lemon grass."

A great believer in food that's healthy as well as flavorful, Samuel also prepares a vegetable napoleon that includes Abaco eggplant, zucchini, roasted red peppers, and whatever else is in season. The vegetables are layered between slices of freshly baked focaccia and drizzled with a green pepper aioli and balsamic reduction.

Loving both the location and the restaurant itself, Samuel has created a true "clubhouse" for the resort's discerning members. The menu changes daily, but several signature dishes, such as Abaco Fish Chowder and the house salad, can be ordered every day of the week. "Our service is impeccable and the food really good, but the feeling and atmosphere are relatively relaxed and informal, especially for the Bahamas," says the chef.

Caramelized Pineapple and White Chocolate Napoleon

THE CLUBHOUSE RESTAURANT AT THE ABACO CLUB ON WINDING BAY,
CHEF SAMUEL FAVELLA

Although there are several parts to this recipe, none is difficult to prepare, and they can all be made in advance and assembled just before serving.

Makes 12 servings

CAKE

2 CUPS (480 ML) ALL-PURPOSE FLOUR, STIRRED
  BEFORE MEASURING

1 TABLESPOON (15 ML) BAKING POWDER

1 TEASPOON (5 ML) SALT

1¼ CUPS (300 ML) SUGAR

½ CUP (120 ML) UNSALTED BUTTER, SOFTENED

2 EGGS

¾ CUP (180 ML) WHOLE MILK

1 TEASPOON (5 ML) PURE VANILLA EXTRACT

PINEAPPLE

UNSALTED BUTTER

2 CORED PINEAPPLES, EACH CUT INTO 12 SLICES

½ CUP (120 ML) PACKED BROWN SUGAR

MOUSSE

8 OUNCES (227 G) BEST-QUALITY WHITE
  CHOCOLATE, SUCH AS VALRHONA OR
  CALLEBAUT

½ CUP (120 ML) SUGAR

½ CUP (120 ML) WATER

3 EGG WHITES

1 CUP (240 ML) HEAVY WHIPPING CREAM

CARAMEL SAUCE

1½ CUPS (360 ML) PACKED BROWN SUGAR

4 TABLESPOONS (60 ML) ALL-PURPOSE FLOUR

1 CUP (240 ML) BOILING WATER

DASH OF SALT

2 TABLESPOONS (30 ML) UNSALTED BUTTER

2 TABLESPOONS (30 ML) HEAVY CREAM

PURE VANILLA EXTRACT

WHITE CHOCOLATE SAUCE

5 OUNCES (142 G) WHITE CHOCOLATE, AT ROOM
  TEMPERATURE

¼ CUP (60 ML) HEAVY CREAM

GARNISH

FRESH MINT SPRIGS

WHITE CHOCOLATE CHUNKS

(CONTINUED)

TO MAKE THE CAKE: Butter and flour a 17" x 12" (43 x 30 cm) jelly roll pan or two 8" x 8" (20 x 20 cm) baking pans. Preheat the oven to 375°F (190°C).

In a small bowl, combine the flour, baking powder, and salt and set aside.

In a large bowl, using an electric mixer on medium speed, cream the sugar and butter, beating until light and fluffy. Add the eggs one at a time, beating well after each addition. Add half the flour mixture, then half the milk. Stir in the vanilla extract and mix until blended. Add the remaining flour and milk and beat until smooth.

Pour the batter into the prepared pan(s) and bake for 17 minutes for a jelly roll pan or for 25 to 35 minutes for 8" x 8" (20 x 20 cm) pans, until the cake springs back when lightly touched near the center. Let cool while preparing the rest of the recipe. If making ahead, cover and refrigerate for up to 2 days.

TO MAKE THE PINEAPPLE: After the cake is done, reduce the oven temperature to 350°F (180°C).

Spread a generous amount of butter onto a large, rimmed baking sheet.

Arrange the pineapple slices on the baking sheet and sprinkle with the brown sugar. Bake for 15 to 20 minutes, turning once or twice until the sugar melts and the edges of the slices are browned. Let cool while preparing the rest of the recipe. If making ahead, remove from the pan and place on a clean baking sheet that has been coated with cooking spray. Cover and refrigerate for up to 2 days.

TO MAKE THE MOUSSE: Chop the chocolate into very small pieces. Place in a microwaveable bowl, and heat on high for about 1 minute, until the chocolate melts. Stir and set aside.

In a medium saucepan, bring the sugar and ½ cup (120 ml) water to a boil, stirring until the sugar dissolves. Remove from the heat. In a medium bowl, using an electric mixer on high speed, beat the egg whites until they form soft peaks. With the mixer running, slowly pour the sugar syrup into the egg whites, and beat for a few minutes longer (the mixture will be loose). Fold in the chocolate and stir well. Let cool to room temperature. Clean the mixing beaters before proceeding to the next step.

In another medium bowl, whip the cream on medium-high speed until soft peaks form. Gently fold into the cooled chocolate mixture, then transfer to a large bowl and refrigerate for at least 2 hours before serving.

TO MAKE THE CARAMEL SAUCE: In a medium saucepan over medium heat, combine the brown sugar and flour and blend well. Add the boiling water and salt and cook, stirring, for 6 to 8 minutes (if the sauce seems too thick, add more water a spoonful at a time). Remove from the heat and stir in the butter, cream, and vanilla extract to taste. Let cool to room temperature. If not using right away, refrigerate and then gently warm mixture to soften when ready to use.

TO MAKE THE WHITE CHOCOLATE SAUCE: Melt the chocolate in a double boiler over hot (not boiling) water for 1 to 2 minutes. Remove from the heat and stir in the cream. Let cool to room temperature. If not using right away, refrigerate and then gently warm mixture to soften when ready to use.

TO ASSEMBLE: Place a caramelized pineapple slice in the center of each dessert plate. Use a cookie cutter to cut 24 rounds of cake, 2 for each serving, and place 1 on top of each pineapple slice. Pipe or spoon a portion of mousse on top of the cake. Stack the layers and garnish each Napoleon with a mint sprig and a small chunk of white chocolate. Pipe or spoon some of each sauce around the edges of each Napoleon.

THE RESTAURANT AT THE COVE

Eleuthera, Bahamas

Owners Scott Bumpas and George Hartley
Executive Chef Ludo Jarland

Eleuthera is one of the more than 700 beautiful and largely undiscovered "out" islands and cays that are the flip side of such busy Bahamian tourist haunts as Paradise Island and Nassau. Originally inhabited by the Arawak Indians, the area where the Cove Resort is now situated was originally named Pineapple Cove because Eleuthera was the first place in the Western Hemisphere to grow and export pineapples. "On the huge pineapple plantations back then, the soil was tilled and crops were planted and harvested by hand, because the terrain was too rough for sophisticated machinery—and that's still done today," says Scott Bumpas, an owner of the Cove Resort. "And although Hawaii is now the pineapple king, there are still quite a few fields around the island."

It's no wonder that one of the best-selling dishes at the Restaurant at the Cove is the Pineapple Tarte Tatin. "This fabulous dessert is similar to a pineapple upside-down cake," explains Executive Chef Ludo Jarland. "Along with fresh Eleuthera pineapple, the ingredients include a caramelized sugar mixture; allspice, also known as Jamaica pepper; and a light and tender pastry."

Raised and schooled in France, Ludo learned his trade from the great chefs at five-star restaurants before finding his way first to Harbour Island and then to Eleuthera. Now he prepares many traditional Bahamian dishes in the classic French manner, with Continental flair. On Wednesdays, his only day off, a Bahamian chef takes over and prepares local favorites such as conch fritters, grouper, peas and rice, and key lime pie.

Another of Ludo's specialties is Coconut French Toast. "There is a woman on the island who makes fresh white bread that we use for our French toast," he says. "I cut the bread into triangles about an inch thick and soak it in eggs, heavy cream, coconut, and vanilla extract until it's soft but not soggy. The bread is then grilled until it's still soft in the middle but crispy outside, and I serve it with real maple syrup and toasted shredded coconut. This is definitely a meal hearty enough to fill up any active water sportsman all day long."

Coconut French Toast

EXECUTIVE CHEF LUDO JARLAND

Makes 4 servings

4 EGGS

¼ CUP (60 ML) SUGAR

1 TEASPOON (5 ML) GROUND CINNAMON

2 CUPS (480 ML) MILK

1 CUP (240 ML) HEAVY CREAM

1 CUP (240 ML) SHREDDED COCONUT

6 SLICES WHITE BREAD, 1" (2.5 CM) THICK, CUT IN HALF ON THE DIAGONAL

½ CUP (120 ML) CLARIFIED BUTTER (SEE NOTE)

TOASTED SHREDDED COCONUT (SEE NOTE)

MAPLE SYRUP

In a large shallow bowl, whisk together the eggs, sugar, and cinnamon. Stir in the milk, cream, and coconut. Add 3 bread slices and soak for 3 to 5 minutes on each side.

Heat 2 tablespoons (30 ml) of the clarified butter in a large nonstick skillet over medium heat until hot but not smoking. Add the bread and cook for 5 minutes on each side, or until golden brown. Soak the remaining bread and cook in the remaining butter.

Arrange 3 pieces of toast on each of 4 plates and sprinkle with the coconut. Serve the maple syrup on the side.

NOTE: *To clarify butter, melt 10 tablespoons (150 ml) unsalted butter in a small saucepan over low heat. Use a spoon to skim off the white frothy layer that forms on the surface as it cooks. When the butter stops frothing, remove from the heat and let settle for a few minutes. Strain through a fine sieve or cheesecloth strainer to remove the milk solids that have formed in the bottom of the skillet. Cover and refrigerate for up to 2 months. Makes ½ cup (120 ml).*

To toast coconut, scatter it on a baking sheet and bake in a 300°F (150°C) oven for 5 to 8 minutes, or until golden and fragrant.

Pineapple Tarte Tatin

EXECUTIVE CHEF LUDO JARLAND

Makes 8 servings

¾ CUP (180 ML) ALL-PURPOSE FLOUR, SIFTED

1 TEASPOON (5 ML) KOSHER SALT

9 TABLESPOONS (135 ML) COLD UNSALTED
   BUTTER, CUT INTO 1" (2.5 CM) CUBES

2 TABLESPOONS (30 ML) VEGETABLE SHORTENING

¼ CUP (60 ML) CAKE FLOUR, SIFTED

½ CUP (120 ML) ICE WATER

¾ CUP (180 ML) SUGAR

½ TEASPOON (2.5 ML) GROUND ALLSPICE

1 PINEAPPLE, PEELED, CORED, AND CUT INTO
   ⅜"-THICK (1 CM) SLICES

In the bowl of a heavy-duty electric mixer fitted with a paddle attachment, mix ½ cup (120 ml) of the flour and the salt. With the mixer on low speed, add 6 tablespoons (90 ml) of the butter and the shortening, a small handful at a time, then increase the speed to medium and mix until completely blended. Stop to scrape down the sides of the bowl as necessary. Reduce the speed to low, add the cake flour and the remaining ¼ cup (60 ml) all-purpose flour, and mix just until combined. Add the water and mix until incorporated. The dough will come up around the paddle and should feel smooth, not sticky, to the touch.

Remove the dough from the mixer and check to be sure there are no visible pieces of butter remaining (mix longer if there are), then form into a ball. Shape into a 7" to 8" (18 cm to 20 cm) disk. Wrap the dough in plastic wrap and refrigerate for at least 2 hours or up to 2 days.

Roll the dough into a circle just slightly larger than a 9" or 10" (23 cm or 25.5 cm) ovenproof skillet. Gently fold in half, then fold again to form a triangle. Transfer to a plate and refrigerate until ready to use.

Spread the sugar in an even layer in the bottom of a skillet. Sprinkle with allspice. Cut the remaining 3 tablespoons (45 ml) butter into 6 pieces and distribute over the sugar. Arrange a circle of pineapple slices in the pan, then add the remaining slices on top of the first layer.

Place the skillet over medium heat to melt the sugar. As it melts, it will combine with the butter and pineapple juice. As the pineapple cooks, the liquid will bubble up around it. It may take up to 45 minutes or more for the caramel to reduce. Because it won't darken once the tarte is in the oven, it must be cooked on the stovetop until it's a very rich, deep brown. When it reaches that color, remove from the heat.

Meanwhile, preheat the oven to 375°F (190°C).

Unfold the dough and drape it around the pineapple, tucking it around the fruit. Bake for 30 to 35 minutes, or until golden brown. Let stand for about 30 minutes so the pineapple absorbs more of the hot caramel.

Invert a serving platter with a lip over the tarte, then carefully invert the tarte onto the platter. Use a paring knife to gently rearrange any pineapple that may be askew. Serve warm.

THE GARDEN TERRACE RESTAURANT AND THE BLUE BAR,

PINK SANDS RESORT

Harbor Island, Bahamas

Manfredi Mancini, Former Executive Chef

The Garden Terrace Restaurant at the Pink Sands Resort is "in the pink" for at least two good reasons. The resort was named the number 4 top Atlantic Ocean resort by readers of *Condé Nast Traveler* in 2005, and the restaurant itself is situated near the resort's renowned 3-mile (4.8-kilometer) stretch of perfect pink sand beach. Decorated in Moroccan, Indonesian, and Balinese style, "the restaurant is warm and inviting," says former executive chef Manfredi Mancini.

The property's other, more casual eating establishment, the Blue Bar, is literally on the beach; known for its fabulous lunches, it can boast of never having an empty table. Manfredi divided the Blue Bar's menu into three sections: Caribbean dishes, chef's choices, and specialties of the Blue Bar. "At lunch, we served all sorts of dishes, from Italian bruschetta and native conch salad to fresh lobster salad made with lobster caught by the Pink Sands' own fisherman. We also made our own lime mayonnaise and served it with garden-grown organic greens and homemade bread.

"There's an à la carte menu for dinner—five entrées that change daily," explains Manfredi. "One of my favorites is the grouper fish, cooked on the grill and served with a fresh tomato, cilantro, onion, and green pepper gazpacho; also, grouper with a radicchio pesto sauce made from the restaurant's organic radicchio, pine nuts, Parmesan cheese, red onion, and extra-virgin olive oil, served on a bed of grilled radicchio."

Manfredi, as his name suggests, was born and raised in Italy. When he was a teenager, he attended culinary school in Capri for 3 years, thus completing his first step toward becoming a chef. His academic training was followed by a globe-trotting 15 years that included a stint as a chef in the army and further international culinary experience in Spain, Portugal, Australia, the Netherlands, and Los Angeles.

Never having had any experience with Caribbean food, Manfredi studied and learned from his predecessor. One of the keys to his success, he says, is keeping it simple, fresh, and flavorful. "With the best fresh ingredients, you don't have to cover the taste with lots of sauces and spices. Once the dish is prepared—that's it!"

Seared Indian-Spiced Scallops and Shrimp

CREATED BY CHEF MANFREDI MANCINI,
PREPARED BY CHEF CLEMENS VON MERVELDT, EXECUTIVE CHEF, GARDEN TERRACE RESTAURANT

Makes 8 servings

SEAFOOD

2 TABLESPOONS (30 ML) MADRAS CURRY POWDER

2 TABLESPOONS (30 ML) MINCED GARLIC

2 TABLESPOONS (30 ML) MINCED FRESH GINGER

2 TABLESPOONS (30 ML) FRESH LIME JUICE

½ CUP (120 ML) + 2 TABLESPOONS (30 ML) OLIVE OIL

24 EXTRA-LARGE SHRIMP, PEELED AND DEVEINED, TAILS REMOVED

24 LARGE SEA SCALLOPS, MUSCLES REMOVED

SALT AND FRESHLY GROUND BLACK PEPPER

GREMOLATA

1 TEASPOON (5 ML) ORANGE ZEST

1 TEASPOON (5 ML) LIME ZEST

¼ CUP (60 ML) CHOPPED FRESH FLAT-LEAF PARSLEY

¼ CUP (60 ML) CHOPPED FRESH CILANTRO

1 TABLESPOON (15 ML) MINCED GARLIC

½ CUP (120 ML) OLIVE OIL

SQUASH CHOKA

¼ CUP (60 ML) OLIVE OIL

1 POUND (454 G) CABOCHA OR BUTTERNUT SQUASH, PEELED AND CHOPPED (ABOUT 3 CUPS [720 ML])

1 TEASPOON (5 ML) MINCED GARLIC

1 TEASPOON (5 ML) MINCED SCOTCH BONNET CHILE PEPPER (SEE NOTE)

½ CUP (120 ML) DICED ONION

2 TEASPOONS (10 ML) CHOPPED FRESH CILANTRO

2 TEASPOONS (10 ML) CHOPPED SCALLION

SALT AND FRESHLY GROUND BLACK PEPPER

TOMATO CHOKA

3 LARGE RIPE TOMATOES, CHARRED OVER AN OPEN FLAME UNTIL SKIN BUBBLES, SKINNED, SEEDED, AND DICED

1 TEASPOON (5 ML) MINCED GARLIC

1 TEASPOON (5 ML) DICED HOT CHILE PEPPER (SEE NOTE)

½ CUP (120 ML) DICED ONION

3 TABLESPOONS (45 ML) OLIVE OIL

2 TEASPOONS (10 ML) CHOPPED FRESH CILANTRO

2 TEASPOONS (10 ML) CHOPPED SCALLION

SALT AND FRESHLY GROUND BLACK PEPPER

(CONTINUED)

BEURRE BLANC

¼ CUP (60 ML) CUMIN SEED

½ CUP (120 ML) WHITE WINE

¼ CUP (60 ML) APPLE CIDER VINEGAR

1 TABLESPOON (15 ML) CHOPPED SCALLION

1 TEASPOON (5 ML) CHOPPED GARLIC

1 TEASPOON (5 ML) CHOPPED FRESH GINGER

1 CUP (240 ML) HEAVY CREAM

1 CUP (240 ML) UNSALTED BUTTER

SALT

TO MAKE THE SEAFOOD: In a stainless steel bowl, whisk together the curry powder, garlic, ginger, lime juice, and the ½ cup (120 ml) oil. Add the shrimp and scallops and refrigerate for 30 minutes.

Heat 1 tablespoon (15 ml) oil in a large skillet over medium-high heat. Remove the shrimp from the marinade and season to taste with the salt and pepper. Add the shrimp, and cook for 2 minutes on each side. Transfer to a bowl and keep warm. Repeat with the scallops using the remaining tablespoon of oil.

TO MAKE THE GREMOLATA: In a small bowl, combine the orange zest, lime zest, parsley, cilantro, garlic, and oil and set aside.

TO MAKE THE SQUASH CHOKA: Heat the oil in a large skillet over medium heat. Add the squash and sauté for 5 to 7 minutes, until tender. Add the garlic, chile pepper, and onion and sauté until the mixture is golden, about 5 minutes. Stir in the cilantro and scallion, and season to taste with the salt and pepper. Remove from the heat and set aside.

TO MAKE THE TOMATO CHOKA: In a medium bowl, combine the tomatoes, garlic, chile pepper, and onion. Heat the oil in a large saucepan over high heat. Carefully pour the tomato mixture over the oil and cook for 3 to 4 minutes, or until the onion begins to brown (do not burn). Remove from the heat and stir in the cilantro and scallion. Season to taste with the salt and pepper.

TO MAKE THE BEURRE BLANC: Toast the cumin seed in a dry pan for a few minutes or just until fragrant (do not burn). Add the wine, vinegar, scallion, garlic, and ginger and cook over medium heat until the liquid is reduced by half. Remove from the heat, strain the seeds from the mixture, and return to the heat. Add the cream and bring to a boil. Reduce the heat to low and whisk in the butter 1 tablespoon (15 ml) at a time, until the sauce is thick and smooth. Season to taste with the salt. Remove from the heat.

TO ASSEMBLE FINISHED DISH: Place small spoonfuls of the two chokas on each plate and the gremolata in the center. Arrange shrimp and scallops around the gremolata, and drizzle with beurre blanc.

NOTE: *Wear plastic gloves when handling Scotch bonnet chiles and chile peppers, and wash your hands thoroughly with soap and water before touching sensitive parts of your body, especially your face. To reduce the heat in the finished dish, use only the sides of the pepper (discard seeds and core).*

Grilled Grouper with Green Pepper Gazpacho

Makes 6 servings

1 LARGE GREEN BELL PEPPER, CORED, SEEDED, AND COARSELY CHOPPED

1 MEDIUM CUCUMBER, COARSELY CHOPPED

1 POUND (454 G) TOMATOES, CHOPPED

1 CUP (240 ML) CHOPPED FRESH CILANTRO

3 CLOVES GARLIC

2 TABLESPOONS (30 ML) VIRGIN OLIVE OIL

1 ONION, CHOPPED

½ CUP (120 ML) TOMATO JUICE

2 TABLESPOONS (30 ML) WHITE WINE VINEGAR

2 TABLESPOONS (30 ML) CRUSHED TOMATOES

1½ POUNDS (680 G) GROUPER FILLET, CUT INTO 1" (2.5 CM) PIECES

SALT AND FRESHLY GROUND BLACK PEPPER

COOKED RICE

LIME SLICES

FRESH DILL

In a blender, combine the peppers, cucumber, tomatoes, cilantro, and garlic and process until thick but not completely smooth.

Heat the oil in a large skillet over medium-high heat. Add the onion and cook for 2 to 3 minutes, until soft. Add the tomato juice, vinegar, and crushed tomatoes, and cook for 2 to 3 minutes longer. Stir in the tomato mixture and heat until bubbling. Reduce the heat and simmer while the grouper cooks.

Heat a stovetop grill to medium-high. Season the fish to taste with the salt and black pepper, and grill for about 5 minutes on each side, or until opaque.

Arrange the fish on a bed of rice and pour the gazpacho over top. Garnish with the lime slices and dill. Serve immediately.

THE CAYMANS

Terrence Howard

From Sea to Beach—
The Taste of Freshness

Acting is in Terrence Howard's blood; his grandmother, Minnie Gentry, was a New York stage actress. Terrence also got his start in New York, appearing on hit television shows such as *Family Matters* and *NYPD Blue* as well as *Living Single, Sparks,* and *Soul Food.* His film credits include roles in *Mr. Holland's Opus, Ray,* and *The Best Man,* a film for which he won an NAACP Image Award as well as nominations for the Chicago Film Critics Association Award and the Independent Spirit Award. In 2005, Terrence's "breakout" year, he appeared in the Academy Award–winning film *Crash* and earned both Golden Globe and Academy Award nominations for his leading role in *Hustle & Flow.*

A Terrence Howard performance is unique and passionate; his connection to the audience, pervasive. When he speaks about his experiences on Grand Cayman, the intensity of his deep emotional connection to the place is clear. The time he's spent on Grand Cayman has been more than a vacation; it's been an apprenticeship, a proving ground. For Terrence, the air there is the breath of life, and to swim in the Cayman waters is to be purified. The only comparison to the simple food he enjoys on the island? Manna from heaven.

It was love that drew Terrence to the Caymans. He spent 3 months there with his then-fiancée when she was Miss Grand Cayman Islands. During that time, he says, he fell in love with everything about the islands as well—the air, the water, the food, and the people.

The Cayman Islands—Grand Cayman, Cayman Brac, and Little Cayman—are located just 180 miles (289.68 kilometers) northwest of Jamaica and are separated from it by the Cayman Trough. Until some time in the 1500s, the islands were nicknamed Lagartos, which means "alligators," perhaps because of the way they appear to rise, humpbacked, from the water, their tricky, reef-edged outer banks just waiting for careless ships or divers to come too close.

For Terrence, the islands' hidden reefs and coves were invitations to test his limits and connect with the spirit of indigenous people who have dived, fished, and sailed there for many centuries. "I heard many wild adventure stories when I was in the Caymans," he says. "My fiancée's grandfather told me about a time when he was stranded at sea and had to swim more than 20 miles (32.19 kilometers) to land. The coral is razor sharp, and there are barracuda in that water, but he did it. To me, that story says a lot about the people of the Caymans. They're resourceful and focused—a gifted group of people—and it shows in everything they do."

Terrence recalls that much of his time in the Caymans was spent in pursuit of food. "My fiancée's brother dove 20 or 30 feet (6.1 or 9.14 meters) down to get conchs in their shells," he recalls excitedly. "There were stingrays down there, and he was putting himself in real danger. But in the Caymans, you can't take queen conchs from the water—they are a protected species—so he ended up returning a lot of them. On the beach, we cut up onions and peppers and a little lime. He cut up the live conch right there and mixed it with the vegetables. We had Conch Ceviche, right then, right there."

Terrence spent time practicing the line-fishing skills he learned from his hosts. These techniques have been used by those native to the island and visiting or marauding tradesmen since before the 1400s. "You have a small bag with your bait—chopped squid—at your side, and a line—just the line with a hook on the end—in your hand, baited with a bit of squid. When a fish took the

bait, we just grabbed it. Then we cleaned the fish and roasted it over a beach fire. There's something about the open fire and how it affects the fish—just very natural and beautiful and, of course, very delicious."

Conventional Caymanian cuisine is strongly influenced by that of nearby Jamaica and includes jerked meats, curries, a variety of rice and peas, root vegetables, and a delicacy that can be found in the coastal waters—turtle.

"Most of the places where we ate, and the foods, were very basic," Terrence says. "Bar Papagayos, where I had jerked pork, was one of them. It was just a little spot where the tables were small and the waitress complained in a good-natured way to make us laugh, but the food was really good.

"The people of the Caymans eat a lot of hot peppers," he says, "but when they're roasted, they're not nearly as hot as you would expect. We'd cook them and eat them with a little homemade sauce. I loved the side dishes, especially fried plantains—I had them at almost every meal." Smiling at the memory, he adds, "You've got me wanting to go back to the Caymans right now!"

GRAND OLD HOUSE RESTAURANT

Grand Cayman Island

Kandathil Mathai, Executive Chef

Reflecting a bit of Old World romance, the Grand Old House is a former coconut plantation set at the edge of the Caribbean Sea. Its world-class executive chef, Kandathil Mathai, has cooked for princes and princesses and lords and ladies as well as presidents and other heads of state, but he is just as honored to prepare sumptuous dishes for the scores of brides and grooms who come to the restaurant to fulfill the "destination wedding" experience of a lifetime. For decades, the Grand Old House has carefully planned and executed every aspect of these events, from securing the marriage licenses and arranging horse-drawn carriage rides to creating the wedding cake every bride dreams of.

If, for Terrence Howard, the Caymans provided an opportunity to find adventure, by contrast, the Grand Old House offers well-appointed luxury that is the antithesis of that experience.

The chef learned his trade at the famed Indian Hotels Company, the Taj Mahal Hotel in Bombay, and the Shangri-la Hotel in Bangkok. He has also worked in Dubai, where he was sous chef for 12 years at the Jebel Ali Hotel and was responsible for suiting the palates of many a royal and dignitary. It's only natural, then, that full-service hospitality is always on the menu at the Grand Old House.

His appointment at the restaurant brought Kandathil and his family to the Caymans, where they have lived happily since 1996. "Indian food is very spicy, but there are differences between Indian spices and those that are typical of the Caribbean—differences, yet many likenesses, too," he says. "Particularly in Bombay, international cuisine was the standard, so coming here to mix Caribbean flavors in a way that would appeal to the majority of our visitors was fairly easy. The guests love the food we offer here. There is one lamb dish in particular that is very much in demand. The Caribbean-influenced flavor comes from the jerk spices we use. Not all jerks are alike, but this one is a perfect blending of several of the spices offered in these islands."

Classic Conch Ceviche the Cayman Way

GRAND OLD HOUSE RESTAURANT, EXECUTIVE CHEF KANDATHIL MATHAI

Makes 4 servings

½ CUP (120 ML) KETCHUP

½ CUP (120 ML) WHITE WINE

½ CUP (120 ML) BLOOD ORANGE JUICE

1 SERRANO OR SCOTCH BONNET CHILE PEPPER, MINCED (SEE NOTE)

1 TEASPOON (5 ML) APPLE CIDER

1 TEASPOON (5 ML) FRESH LIME JUICE

1 TEASPOON (5 ML) PICKAPEPPA SAUCE (SEE RESOURCES, PAGE 245)

1 TEASPOON (5 ML) WORCESTERSHIRE SAUCE

1 TEASPOON (5 ML) CRUSHED BLACK PEPPER

SALT

1 POUND (454 G) FRESH CONCH

3 SMALL BELL PEPPERS, ASSORTED COLORS, CUT INTO MATCHSTICK SLICES

1 SMALL RIB CELERY, CUT INTO MATCHSTICK SLICES

1 SMALL BUNCH FRESH CILANTRO, CHOPPED

2 SCALLIONS, SLICED

FRESH LETTUCE LEAVES

PLANTAIN CHIPS

In a large bowl, whisk together the ketchup, wine, orange juice, chile pepper, cider, lime juice, pickapeppa sauce, Worcestershire sauce, and black pepper. Season to taste with salt.

Wash the conch several times in cold water and pat dry. Slice into very fine slivers and add to the ketchup mixture, then add the bell peppers, celery, cilantro, and scallions. Toss gently to combine. Let stand for 30 minutes before serving on a bed of lettuce, garnished with plantain chips.

NOTE: *Wear plastic gloves when handling Scotch bonnet chiles, and wash your hands thoroughly with soap and water before touching sensitive parts of your body, especially your face. To reduce the heat in the finished dish, use only the sides of the pepper (discard seeds and core).*

Ginger-Sesame Seared Yellow-Fin Tuna with Arugula Coulis, Tropical Fruit Chutney, and Soy Drizzle

GRAND OLD HOUSE RESTAURANT, EXECUTIVE CHEF KANDATHIL MATHAI

Makes 4 servings

TUNA

2 TEASPOONS (10 ML) KEY LIME JUICE

½ CUP (120 ML) SOY SAUCE

¾ CUP (180 ML) SESAME OIL

SALT AND FRESHLY GROUND BLACK PEPPER

4 CENTER-CUT YELLOW-FIN TUNA STEAKS, 8 OUNCES (227 G) EACH

2 TEASPOONS (10 ML) MIXED BLACK AND WHITE SESAME SEEDS

1 TABLESPOON (15 ML) CHOPPED FRESH GINGER

COULIS

¼ CUP (60 ML) WHITE WINE

¾ CUP (180 ML) FINELY CHOPPED ONION

½ TABLESPOON (7.5 ML) CHOPPED FRESH GINGER

¼ CUP (60 ML) COCONUT MILK

1 RED CHILE PEPPER, CHOPPED

1 BUNCH ARUGULA

1 TABLESPOON (15 ML) FRESH LIME JUICE

1 TABLESPOON (15 ML) UNSALTED BUTTER

SALT AND FRESHLY GROUND BLACK PEPPER

CHUTNEY

1 CAN (8 OUNCES [227 G]) MIXED TROPICAL FRUIT, WITH SYRUP

2 CINNAMON STICKS

2 TABLESPOONS (30 ML) CHOPPED FRESH MINT

1 TEASPOON (5 ML) CORNSTARCH

1 TABLESPOON (15 ML) WATER

SOY DRIZZLE

1 CUP (240 ML) FISH STOCK

¼ CUP (60 ML) WHITE WINE

¼ CUP (60 ML) SOY SAUCE

½ TABLESPOON (7.5 ML) CHOPPED FRESH GINGER

1 TABLESPOON (15 ML) SUGAR

2 TEASPOONS (10 ML) CORNSTARCH

1 TABLESPOON (15 ML) WATER

TO PREPARE THE TUNA: In a large bowl, combine the lime juice, soy sauce, and ½ cup (120 ml) of the sesame oil and season to taste with the salt and pepper. Add the tuna, turning to coat all sides, then refrigerate for 1 hour. In a shallow bowl, combine the sesame seeds and ginger, then roll the tuna in the mixture until well coated. Set aside for 20 minutes while preparing the rest of the recipe.

TO MAKE THE COULIS: Half-fill a medium saucepan with water and bring to a gentle boil over high heat.

In another medium saucepan over medium heat, combine the wine, onion, and ginger and bring to a boil. Cook for about 5 minutes, or until the liquid is reduced by half. Reduce the heat, add the coconut milk and chile pepper, and simmer for about 5 minutes.

Meanwhile, place the arugula in the boiling water for 1 minute, then drain. Transfer to a food processor and process with on/off pulses until smooth. Add to the coconut mixture, increase the heat, and bring to a boil for 1 minute. Whisk in the lime juice and butter, then strain. Season to taste with the salt and pepper. Keep warm until ready to serve.

TO MAKE THE CHUTNEY: In a small saucepan over medium heat, combine the fruit, cinnamon sticks, and mint. Bring to a boil, then reduce the heat and simmer for 10 minutes.

In a small bowl, combine the cornstarch and water and stir until smooth. Add to the pan, stirring gently until thick. Remove from the heat and set aside. Discard the cinnamon sticks and mint before serving.

TO MAKE THE SOY DRIZZLE: In a saucepan over high heat, combine the stock, wine, soy sauce, ginger, and sugar. Bring to a boil and cook for 2 minutes.

In a small bowl, combine the cornstarch and water and stir until smooth. Add to the soy sauce mixture and cook until beginning to thicken. Remove from the heat and keep warm.

TO COOK THE TUNA AND ASSEMBLE: Heat the remaining ¼ cup (60 ml) oil in a large skillet over medium-high heat until very hot. Add the tuna and sear for 1 to 2 minutes on each side. Streak each plate with the coulis, chutney, and soy drizzle and arrange the tuna on top. Serve with rice or mashed potatoes, if desired.

Jerk-Spiced Herb-Crusted Rack of Baby Lamb with Smoky Carrot-Lamb au Jus

GRAND OLD HOUSE RESTAURANT, EXECUTIVE CHEF KANDATHIL MATHAI

Makes 4 servings

LAMB

½ CUP (120 ML) CARIBBEAN JERK SEASONING

2 TEASPOONS (10 ML) WORCESTERSHIRE SAUCE

5 CLOVES GARLIC, CHOPPED

½ CUP (120 ML) + 2 TABLESPOONS (30 ML) OLIVE OIL

SALT AND FRESHLY GROUND BLACK PEPPER

4 FRENCHED RACKS OF BABY LAMB, ABOUT 10 OUNCES (283 G) EACH

½ LOAF FRESH COUNTRY WHITE BREAD

1 CUP (240 ML) CHOPPED MIXED FRESH BASIL, ROSEMARY, PARSLEY, MINT, AND THYME

½ CUP (120 ML) COARSE MUSTARD

AU JUS

¼ CUP (60 ML) RED WINE

1½ CUPS (360 ML) CARROT JUICE

1 CUP (240 ML) BEEF OR LAMB STOCK

1 TABLESPOON (15 ML) FRESH ROSEMARY

4 TABLESPOONS (60 ML) BUTTER

2–3 DROPS LIQUID SMOKE

TO MAKE THE LAMB: In a pan large enough to hold all the lamb, combine the jerk seasoning, Worcestershire sauce, half the garlic, the ½ cup (120 ml) oil, and salt and pepper to taste. Add the lamb, turning to coat on all sides, and let stand for 1 hour. Meanwhile, preheat the oven to 350°F (180°C).

Break up the bread and place in a food processor along with the mixed herbs, remaining garlic, and 1 tablespoon (15 ml) oil. Process until it forms a thick paste.

Heat the remaining 1 tablespoon (15 ml) of oil in a nonstick pan over medium-high heat, and pan-fry the lamb just until golden brown on all sides. Remove from the heat. When it has cooled slightly, rub the tops of the racks with the mustard and the herb mixture. Transfer to a roasting pan, meat side up, and roast for 15 minutes, or until a thermometer inserted into the center registers 145°F (63°C) for medium-rare. Remove from the oven and cover loosely with aluminum foil. Let stand for 10 minutes before slicing.

TO MAKE THE AU JUS: In a stockpot over medium heat, combine the wine, carrot juice, stock, and rosemary and cook for 10 minutes, or until reduced by half. Strain, then whisk in the butter, adding the liquid smoke at the end. Serve with the lamb.

JAMAICA

Alicia Keys

IRIE MUSIC AND A BLESSED LIFE

Alicia Keys has been writing songs since she was 14 years old. A native of Manhattan, Alicia graduated from the Professional Performing Arts School and entered Columbia University at the age of 16. Her debut album, *Songs in A Minor,* which she wrote and produced with the guidance of her manager, Jeff Robinson, for Clive Davis's newly minted J Records label, sold more than 50,000 copies its first day on sale. Her next release, *Diary of Alicia Keys,* sold more than 600,000 copies in the first week and brought even more acclaim to the young talent. Both of these albums, as well as her recently released *Unplugged* album, debuted at number 1. Now in her midtwenties, Alicia has already experienced what for most people would be more than a lifetime's worth of success.

Critics and fans alike have hailed Alicia Keys as the crest of the wave in the "rebirth of real music for the modern culture." Alicia has experienced a rebirth of her own in coming up from Hell's Kitchen to the world's most prominent stages and arenas. This has surely helped mold her into the socially conscious, unaffected young woman that she is today—eager to give back to young fans who look to her for inspiration.

She has spent time in Jamaica both appearing with her band and just sitting by the pool in Montego Bay to regain her inner peace. Integral to those experiences was the outright joy of eating the island's freshly caught fish and drinking freshly squeezed tropical fruit juices. When talking about the foods and flavors of this beautiful island, it's obvious that Alicia really loves to eat!

"I don't drink coffee, but coffee drinkers love that Blue Mountain, don't they?" says Alicia, referring to Jamaica's second most famous beverage export—the first, of course, being rum. While she may not have savored the flavor of the island's justly famous high-peak coffee beans, the multitalented singer/songwriter is clearly enamored of other Jamaican cultural and culinary delights.

The third largest of the Caribbean islands, Jamaica is a musical Mecca for some of the world's

greatest performers, whose creative juices are fed by the ska, British, reggae, and soul music cultures that have flourished there for decades. And the voices of masters such as Bob Marley, Toots Hibbert, and Jimmy Cliff beckon to artists like Alicia, who are eager to mix a variety of rhythms and traditions.

"I usually have a performance in Jamaica when I'm there," she says. "But then I stay on for a few days. I write some music, but mostly I just read and run on the beach. Sometimes my band will go to a waterslide there—they love that place! But in Jamaica, I just want to be at ease.

"The Half Moon in Montego Bay is where I always end up," she continues, referring to the exclusive luxury resort situated on the island's North Coast. Despite the six first-rate restaurants on the property, Alicia prefers to eat in her own villa. "We'll have a

cook—somebody from the area who comes in. The people are so nice that I really feel as if I'm staying with family."

Next to the warmth and care, what Alicia appreciates most is the food. Just the memory of eating a particular kind of dumpling is enough to elicit a blissful moan. "I don't know how they prepare them, but they are *so good!* And ackee—a Jamaican fruit—with salt fish! I love the ackee and salt fish in Jamaica. It's like no place else, just perfectly rich and savory.

"I don't eat chicken or meat, but the folks I travel with do. Sometimes at the villa, they cook out on the patio—all day long." For those who eat meat, that means smoky, familiar smells and the anticipation of a fabulous barbecue. Barbecue in Jamaica means juicy jerk chicken, sausage, flavorful goat, and grilled fish.

"I love the red snapper dishes I've had in Jamaica," Alicia says. "The fish is just so fresh. And then there's this great fruit punch, made from scratch—full of fresh, flavorful tropical juices. It's so good."

Although the Half Moon Resort offers a sanctuary for restoring her creativity and resting after a hectic performance schedule, Alicia is acutely aware of the poverty that pervades the island. "The poverty is very obvious there—it reminds me of places I've seen in Africa. But even if the people's situation is dire, they always seem to look at the positive and talk about being blessed."

Jamaican Pepper Shrimp
with Wasabi Mashed Potatoes and Ackee Sauce

HALF MOON RESORT, EXECUTIVE CHEF FREDRICK GAYLE

Makes 6 servings

SHRIMP

4 TABLESPOONS (60 ML) VEGETABLE OIL

2 CUPS (480 ML) DICED SEEDED GREEN BELL PEPPERS

1 CUP (240 ML) DICED ONION

1 CUP (240 ML) DICED TOMATOES

2 TEASPOONS (10 ML) FRESH THYME

SALT AND FRESHLY GROUND BLACK PEPPER

1½ POUNDS (681 G) SHRIMP, PEELED AND DEVEINED, TAILS REMOVED

2 TABLESPOONS (30 ML) CHOPPED GARLIC

1 SCOTCH BONNET CHILE PEPPER, DICED (SEE NOTE)

½ CUP (120 ML) BRANDY

POTATOES

1½ POUNDS (681 G) POTATOES, PEELED AND CUT INTO 1" (2.5 CM) CHUNKS

1 TEASPOON (5 ML) SALT + ADDITIONAL FOR SEASONING

1 CUP (240 ML) MILK

2 TABLESPOONS (30 ML) UNSALTED BUTTER

1 TABLESPOON (15 ML) WASABI POWDER

FRESHLY GROUND BLACK PEPPER

SAUCE

1 TEASPOON (5 ML) OLIVE OIL

1 CUP (240 ML) DICED ONION

2 TABLESPOONS (30 ML) CHOPPED GARLIC

1 TABLESPOON (15 ML) FRESH THYME

1 CAN (20 OUNCES [567 G]) ACKEE, STRAINED (SEE RESOURCES, PAGE 245)

1 CUP (240 ML) CHICKEN STOCK

1 CUP (240 ML) HEAVY CREAM

TO MAKE THE SHRIMP: Heat 2 tablespoons (30 ml) of the oil in a large skillet over medium-high heat. Add the bell peppers and onion and cook for about 12 minutes, or until soft. Add the tomatoes, thyme, and salt and pepper to taste, then reduce the heat and simmer for 10 minutes.

Meanwhile, heat the remaining 2 tablespoons (30 ml) oil in another large skillet over medium-high heat. Add the shrimp, garlic, and chile peppers and cook for about 3 minutes, or until the shrimp turn pink. Season to taste with the salt. Remove the pan from the heat and add the brandy (do not pour straight from the bottle). Return to heat. If desired, use a long match to carefully light the brandy (stand away from the pan as flames may shoot upward). If you choose not to flambé, cook off the added brandy for 2 to 3 minutes before adding the vegetable mixture to the shrimp.

TO MAKE THE POTATOES: Place the potatoes in a medium saucepan and add the 1 teaspoon (5 ml) salt and enough cold water to cover. Bring to a gentle boil over high heat and cook for 15 to 20 minutes, or until tender. Drain in a colander. Heat the milk and butter in the same pan until the butter melts, then remove from the heat and return the potatoes to the pan. Add the wasabi. Beat with a potato masher or handheld blender until smooth, then season to taste with the pepper.

TO MAKE THE SAUCE: In a large saucepan, heat the oil over medium-high heat. Add the onion, garlic, thyme, and ackee, and sauté for 5 minutes until the vegetables soften. Add the chicken stock and heavy cream, reduce heat to simmer, and cook until reduced by half.

Puree the mixture with a handheld blender until smooth.

NOTE: *Wear plastic gloves when handling Scotch bonnet chiles, and wash your hands thoroughly with soap and water before touching sensitive parts of your body, especially your face. To reduce the heat in the finished dish, use only the sides of the pepper (discard seeds and core).*

Salt-Fish Fritters

HALF MOON RESORT, EXECUTIVE CHEF FREDRICK GAYLE

Makes 36

½ POUND (227 G) SALTED CODFISH

6 SCALLIONS, CHOPPED

½ CUP (120 ML) CHOPPED FRESH PARSLEY

2 CUPS (480 ML) DICED SEEDED GREEN BELL
   PEPPERS

2 CLOVES GARLIC, MINCED

1 SCOTCH BONNET CHILE PEPPER, SEEDED AND
   MINCED (SEE NOTE)

1 CUP (240 ML) ALL-PURPOSE FLOUR

2 TEASPOONS (10 ML) BAKING POWDER

2 EGGS

½ CUP (120 ML) MILK

VEGETABLE OIL

Place the fish in a large bowl with enough water to cover, and refrigerate for 24 hours, rinsing the fish and exchanging the water three times.

Add the fish to a large pot of water, bring to a boil, reduce heat, and simmer for 20 to 25 minutes. Rinse with cold water, remove the skin and bones, and flake into a large bowl. Add the scallions, parsley, bell peppers, garlic, and chile pepper and toss gently to combine.

In another large bowl, whisk together the flour, baking powder, eggs, and milk (the mixture will be slightly lumpy). Add the fish mixture and stir until thoroughly combined.

Heat at least 2" (5 cm) of oil in a large pot over medium-high heat, until the temperature reaches 350°F (180°C). Working in batches, slip tablespoon-size (15 ml) portions of the fritter mixture into the oil, and fry for 5 minutes, or until golden. Transfer to paper towels to drain.

NOTE: *Wear plastic gloves when handling Scotch bonnet chiles, and wash your hands thoroughly with soap and water before touching sensitive parts of your body, especially your face. To reduce the heat in the finished dish, use only the sides of the pepper (discard seeds and core).*

Squash–Sweet Potato Puree

HALF MOON RESORT, EXECUTIVE CHEF FREDRICK GAYLE

This delicious puree comes by its sweetness naturally. Just a hint of ginger and nutmeg makes it a wonderful accompaniment to many traditional island dishes, such as Escovitched Snapper or Rundown.

Makes 10 servings

2 POUNDS (1 KG) CABOCHA OR BUTTERNUT SQUASH, PEELED AND CUT INTO 1" (2.5 CM) PIECES

2 POUNDS (1 KG) SWEET POTATOES, PEELED AND CUT INTO 1" (2.5 CM) PIECES

½ CUP (120 ML) MILK

2 TABLESPOONS (30 ML) GRATED FRESH GINGER

½ TEASPOON (2.5 ML) GRATED NUTMEG

SALT AND FRESHLY GROUND BLACK PEPPER

Place the squash and sweet potatoes in a large saucepan and add enough cold water to cover. Bring to a gentle boil over high heat and cook for approximately 10 minutes, or until tender.

Meanwhile, in a small saucepan over medium heat, combine the milk, ginger, and nutmeg and bring to a simmer.

When the vegetables are cooked, drain, return to the pan, add the milk mixture, and beat with a potato masher or handheld mixer until smooth. Season to taste with the salt and pepper.

Rum-Raisin Ice Cream

HALF MOON RESORT, EXECUTIVE CHEF FREDRICK GAYLE

Makes 1 quart

½ CUP (120 ML) RAISINS

¼ CUP (60 ML) DARK JAMAICAN RUM

3 CUPS (720 ML) HEAVY OR WHIPPING CREAM

1 CUP (240 ML) MILK

½ CUP (120 ML) SUGAR

½ TEASPOON (2.5 ML) GROUND NUTMEG

1 TABLESPOON (15 ML) PURE VANILLA EXTRACT

4 EGG YOLKS

In a small bowl, soak the raisins in the rum for 30 minutes.

In a large heavy saucepan over medium heat, combine the cream, milk, sugar, nutmeg, and vanilla extract. Cook for about 10 minutes, or until the milk is hot but not boiling and the sugar is dissolved, then remove from the heat.

In a medium bowl, beat the egg yolks. Slowly pour in 1 cup (240 ml) of the milk mixture, whisking constantly until smooth. Slowly pour into the pan, whisking constantly until well combined. Return to medium heat and stir constantly until the mixture is thick enough to coat the back of a spoon, about 5 minutes (do not boil). Strain into a large bowl, cover the surface of the custard with plastic wrap to keep a skin from forming, and let cool to room temperature.

Strain the raisins, reserving the rum. Stir the rum into the custard. Freeze in an ice cream maker according to manufacturer's directions. Five minutes before the ice cream is finished, stir in the raisins, then complete the freezing process.

Ben Vereen

JAMMIN' IN JAMAICA

After appearing in the touring company of *Sweet Charity* and on Broadway in *Hair* and *Jesus Christ Superstar*, multitalented Ben Vereen proved his dramatic ability portraying Chicken George in the history-making television miniseries *Roots*, a role for which he received an Emmy nomination. His Broadway triumphs include *Pippin* (for which he won both Tony and Drama Desk Awards) and unforgettable appearances in *Fosse*, *Chicago*, and *Jelly's Last Jam*, to name just a few. In 1978, with his television special *Ben Vereen . . . His Roots*, he added the Emmy to his collection. The versatile Mr. Vereen's most recent triumph was in the Tony Award–winning production of *Wicked*.

But life has not always been so good. At the height of his career, Ben was felled by a serious automobile accident that was compounded when he was released from the hospital with a closed head injury, became disoriented, and was struck by a car traveling on Pacific Coast Highway.

Taking almost a decade to fully recover, Ben was honored with the Achievement in Excellence Award in 2004 from his alma mater, the renowned High School of the Performing Arts. As widely honored for his humanitarian activities as for his stage appearances, Ben received Israel's Humanitarian Award in 1990, was honored with the NAACP's prestigious Image Awards in 1987, and founded his own organization, Celebrities for a Drug Free America, in the early '90s.

Ben has an almost magical and mystical connection to Jamaica, first visiting the island in 1971 when he badly needed a bit of rest and relaxation after he had, as he put it, "pretty much exhausted" himself preparing for the opening of *Pippin.* Since then, he's been back many times, learning about Rastafarian music and culture and enjoying their simple but eminently satisfying ways with food. He loves not only the people and culture of Jamaica but also the fresh "straight from the garden or tree" fruits and vegetables that are so compatible with his vegan lifestyle.

On his initial visit, he says, "A friend of mine who plays the cello flew down with me. We stayed at Montego Bay, and at night he would play and I would dance along the beach."

His next visit was several years later, when he was asked by Michael Butler, producer of *Hair,* to create a show called *Reggae.* On that trip, he says, "I traveled up into the hills to visit the Rastafarians. I wanted to find out about the music from Bali, Africa, and the different Rasta sects. Hanging out with the local poets and musicians, I learned about their culture and about the Africans who were brought to Jamaica and how their music kept them alive and vital. That's when I met a guy who was singing about the slums of Jamaica. I was so impressed that I decided to put his music in my act. His name is Bob Marley."

Back then, Ben was not yet a vegan, so he had no problem feasting on jerk chicken or freshly caught fish that were cooked right in front of him on the beach while the Rastafarians played their drums, danced, and sang. Many Rastafarians don't eat food that isn't freshly killed, because eating anything that's already dead goes against the beliefs of their tribal fathers.

Now that Ben is a vegan, Jamaica's bounty still provides him with plenty to feast on "straight out of the garden."

Although he's a great believer in the benefits of raw foods, he says that in Jamaica, "the produce is so fresh and tree or vine ripened that even slightly steamed, the broccoli, corn, and breadfruit are sweet and flavorful."

On his most recent visit, Ben spent a week at the beautiful Villa Monzon, located in a private community of seven homes overlooking Montego Bay, where he relaxed and reflected on a life full of challenges and successes. "The several days I spent at the villa passed too quickly, but I enjoyed sunning on the roof, swimming in the beautiful pool, and going down to the village to listen to an

amazing steel-drum jazz band. I even found several empty beaches where I could walk alone on the sand for hours at a time.

"The chef prepared some very, very nice vegan meals for me. Going a step beyond vegetarian, vegan dishes are prepared without dairy, eggs, or any food products that come from animals. The Jamaican spices, from cumin and curry to rich cinnamon, are so distinct that well-prepared traditional vegan dishes are especially tasty and filling."

One of Ben's favorite Villa Monzon meals was Chef Christopher Walker's Ital Soup, a hearty blend of such starchy vegetables as yams, sweet potatoes, pumpkin, chayote squash, and carrots, all simmered together with plenty of freshly ground black pepper.

"Jamaican cuisine is not fancy," says Ben, "but when I am there, I always feel the Rasta influence of fresh and flavorful food along with a melting pot of fragrant spices from Africa to India. This island is truly a garden of edible bounties that I feast upon every time I visit."

Chris's Ital Soup

VILLA MONZON, CHEF CHRISTOPHER WALKER

A healthy and hearty soup that is truly satisfying, whether you are vegetarian or not, this dish is an original "Ital" feast.

Makes 6 servings

1 POUND (454 G) YAMS (ABOUT 2 MEDIUM), CUT INTO 2" (5 CM) PIECES

½ POUND (227 G) SWEET POTATOES (1 MEDIUM, CUT INTO 2" [5 CM] PIECES)

1 CAN COCONUT MILK

3 CUPS (720 ML) VEGETABLE BROTH

1 POUND (454 G) FRESH PUMPKIN OR BUTTERNUT SQUASH, PEELED AND CUT INTO 2" (5 CM) PIECES

½ POUND (227 G) CARROTS (3 MEDIUM), PEELED AND SLICED

1 POUND (454 G) FRESH CALLALOO, OR 1 CAN (19 OUNCES [538 G]) CALLALOO, DRAINED; OR ½ POUND (227 G) SPINACH AND ½ POUND (227 G) KALE

1 CHAYOTE SQUASH

1 GREEN PEPPER

2 MEDIUM-SIZED TOMATOES

2 CLOVES GARLIC

3 SPRING ONIONS OR SCALLIONS

5–6 CUPS (1.2–1.4 L) SHREDDED CABBAGE

1 HOT PEPPER, MINCED

FRESHLY GROUND BLACK PEPPER AND SALT

Place the yams and sweet potatoes in a stockpot with the coconut milk and broth.

Add the pumpkin or squash and the carrots.

Bring to a boil and simmer for 10 minutes.

While the root vegetables simmer, carefully wash the callaloo, trimming away any thick stems. Chop and set aside.

To peel the chayote squash, cut it lengthwise into quarters and remove the heart. Dice the remaining squash, green pepper, tomatoes, garlic, and spring onions, and add with the shredded cabbage and hot pepper to the stockpot.

Simmer for 20 minutes more until the vegetables are tender. Season with plenty of freshly ground black pepper and salt if desired. Puree the vegetables for a richer soup.

Jamaican Curried Tofu

CHEF MARCIA LEWIS

Makes 4 servings

1 POUND (454 G) FIRM TOFU

BRAGG LIQUID AMINO OR LIGHT SOY SAUCE

SALT AND FRESHLY GROUND BLACK PEPPER

½ TEASPOON (2.5 ML) GROUND CUMIN

¼ TEASPOON (1.2 ML) GARLIC POWDER

¼ TEASPOON (1.2 ML) JAMAICAN CURRY POWDER

2–3 TABLESPOONS (30–45 ML) OLIVE OIL, OR
    MORE AS NEEDED

1 MEDIUM ONION, DICED

1 MEDIUM POTATO, PEELED AND CUT INTO
    ½" (1.25 CM) CUBES

¾ CUP (180 ML) BABY CARROTS

1 MEDIUM ROMA TOMATO, DICED

2 SCALLIONS, CHOPPED

5 SPRIGS FRESH THYME

½ TEASPOON (2.5 ML) GROUND ALLSPICE

1 CUP (240 ML) WATER

1 VEGETARIAN BOUILLON CUBE

1 TABLESPOON (15 ML) FLOUR DISSOLVED IN
    3 TABLESPOONS (45 ML) WATER

1 TABLESPOON (15 ML) EACH DICED SEEDED RED
    AND GREEN BELL PEPPER, FOR GARNISH

FRESH THYME SPRIGS, FOR GARNISH

Drain the tofu and slice into 8 to 10 pieces. Sprinkle both sides lightly with the Liquid Amino and season to taste with the salt, black pepper, cumin, garlic powder, and curry powder. Heat the oil in a large skillet over medium-high heat, add the tofu, and fry on both sides until firm and golden. Transfer to a plate and set aside.

Add more oil to the skillet if needed, then add the onion, potato, and carrots and sauté until tender. Season with a pinch of salt and add the tomato, scallions, thyme, allspice, 1 cup (240 ml) water, and bouillon. Bring to a boil, then add the flour and water mixture and cook until the sauce begins to thicken. Return the tofu to the skillet and simmer for approximately 10 minutes. Serve garnished with the bell peppers and thyme sprigs.

THE GAZEBO

Goldeneye, Ochos Rios

Pamela Clarke, Executive Chef
Jenny Wood, Food Manager

"Vacation like James Bond," raves the Travel Channel about the Goldeneye, an extraordinary villa resort near Ochos Rios whose Main House was once the home of Ian Fleming.

In fact, Fleming wrote 14 of his James Bond thrillers in the master villa that still looks very much as it did in the 1940s, when Bond's creator entertained famous guests, including Errol Flynn, Elizabeth Taylor, and Truman Capote.

At Goldeneye, guests "still feel like they are in the home of a good friend," says food manager Jenny Woods. "We really like people to share a true Jamaican cultural experience, and we encourage our staff to maintain their own personalities but also to perform at a very high level of service. We offer simple and understated luxury in perfect harmony with the resort's natural surroundings."

Pamela Clarke, executive chef at Goldeneye's Gazebo Restaurant, was born and raised on Jamaica. She learned to cook from her mother and grandmother and prides herself on creating dishes much like the ones Jamaican grandmothers still prepare at home. "Many of the dishes I serve have been handed down from generation to generation," she says. "One of my favorites is Jamaica Jerk Chicken. We make our own jerk seasonings with allspice, black pepper, thyme, garlic—all natural seasonings. We marinate the chicken overnight with these dry ingredients and the next day cook it on the barbecue. The smoke coming from the grill gives the meat a savory flavor. And the sweet potatoes and baked plantains that go with it are just as good.

"Our emphasis is on authentic Jamaican cuisine," Jenny adds. "We buy our fish fresh from the local fishermen every single morning. Each dish is created daily. We look at our guest list and work out a menu so we don't prepare the same food twice during any guest's stay."

Racecourse Fish in Rundown

THE GAZEBO, EXECUTIVE CHEF PAMELA CLARKE

Makes 6 servings

6 RED SNAPPER FILLETS, 8 OUNCES (227 G) EACH

SALT AND FRESHLY GROUND BLACK PEPPER

1 CAN (13½ OUNCES [400 ML]) COCONUT MILK (NOT LITE)

2 SCALLIONS, CHOPPED

2 SPRIGS FRESH THYME, CHOPPED

1 MEDIUM ONION, CHOPPED

3 CLOVES GARLIC, CHOPPED

1 SMALL SCOTCH BONNET CHILE PEPPER, CHOPPED (SEE NOTE)

6 ALLSPICE BERRIES, CRUSHED

2 MEDIUM TOMATOES, CHOPPED

2 TABLESPOONS (30 ML) VEGETABLE OIL

Wash and dry the fish, season to taste with the salt and pepper, and set aside.

In a large saucepan over medium heat, bring the coconut milk to a simmer. Stir in the scallions, thyme, onion, garlic, chile pepper, allspice, and tomatoes. Reduce the heat to low and simmer for at least 10 minutes.

Meanwhile, heat the oil in a large nonstick skillet over medium-high heat until hot but not smoking. Slip the fish into the pan and sear quickly on both sides, but do not cook completely. Lower heat to medium and continue cooking the fish for another 3 to 5 minutes, until it flakes easily. Spoon the sauce onto a large serving platter and place the cooked fillets on top. Serve each fillet with sauce spooned over the top, with any combination of roasted yams, boiled green bananas, dumplings, and callaloo or rice.

NOTE: *Wear plastic gloves when handling Scotch bonnet chiles, and wash your hands thoroughly with soap and water before touching sensitive parts of your body, especially your face. To reduce the heat in the finished dish, use only the sides of the pepper (discard seeds and core).*

Miss Pam's Jamaica Jerk Chicken

THE GAZEBO, EXECUTIVE CHEF PAMELA CLARKE

Makes 8 servings

2–3 BUNCHES SCALLIONS, FINELY CHOPPED

6 LARGE CLOVES GARLIC, FINELY CHOPPED

1–2 SCOTCH BONNET CHILE PEPPERS, FINELY
    CHOPPED (SEE NOTE)

2 TABLESPOONS (30 ML) DRIED THYME

2 TABLESPOONS (30 ML) GROUND ALLSPICE

2–3 TABLESPOONS (30–45 ML) BROWN SUGAR

¼ CUP (60 ML) LIME JUICE

½ CUP (120 ML) VEGETABLE OIL

2 CHICKENS (3½ POUNDS [1.6 KG] EACH),
    WASHED, PATTED DRY, AND QUARTERED

SALT AND FRESHLY GROUND BLACK PEPPER

½ CUP (120 ML) KETCHUP

In a large bowl, combine the scallions, garlic, chile pepper, thyme, allspice, brown sugar, lime juice, and oil, and let stand for at least 1 hour. Rub the chicken pieces with salt and pepper to taste, place in a deep bowl, and add the marinade, lightly massaging the chicken to force the marinade under the skin. Cover and refrigerate for at least 2 hours or overnight.

Preheat the grill. Remove the chicken from the marinade, scraping off and reserving the excess. Place the chicken on the grill and cook, basting with the marinade, until golden brown on both sides. Reduce the heat and cook, basting and turning, for approximately 1 hour, or until cooked through.

To make a sauce, strain the leftover marinade and place in a medium saucepan over medium-high heat. Bring to a boil. Reduce the heat to a simmer, add the ketchup, and cook until the mixture reaches the consistency of barbecue sauce.

When the chicken is cooked, chop into bite-size pieces. Serve with rice and peas, fried plantains, and a green vegetable, if desired, with the sauce on the side.

NOTE: *Wear plastic gloves when handling Scotch bonnet chiles, and wash your hands thoroughly with soap and water before touching sensitive parts of your body, especially your face. To reduce the heat in the finished dish, use only the sides of the pepper (discard seeds and core).*

TURKS AND CAICOS

Ben Affleck

JUST BEING THERE

Ben Affleck has been acting since he was in elementary school but came to serious notice as a young teen when he costarred in the ABC Afterschool Special *Wanted: The Perfect Guy* in 1986. He went on to play the adolescent heavy in films such as *School Ties* and *Dazed and Confused* and to star in filmmaker Kevin Smith's *Mallrats* and *Chasing Amy.*

His career really took off, however, when he and his childhood friend Matt Damon collaborated on the screenplay for *Good Will Hunting,* in which they also starred and for which they won an Academy Award for Best Original Screenplay. Following that success, Ben has gone on to star in films such as *Armageddon, Shakespeare in Love, Pearl Harbor,* and *The Sum of All Fears.*

In addition, he and Matt Damon have continued to work together behind the camera as creators of the television series *Push Nevada* as well as *Project Greenlight,* which started as an Internet screenwriting competition and became an HBO series.

For someone whose life is so busy and often so public, a vacation in the Caribbean is an opportunity to kick back and relax. Although he loves "everything Caribbean," the one place Ben returns to again and again is the Parrot Cay Resort. Maybe it's happy memories that draw him back—or maybe it's the decadently delicious Chocolate Hazelnut Cake served at the resort's Lotus restaurant.

The Turks and Caicos are among the most beautiful islands in the world, with alabaster sand and water so transparent that, as Ben puts it, "even at 8 feet deep, you can read the pages of a book." A certified diver, he loves snorkeling in those waters, where "the coral reefs are so close to the surface that you can see the extraordinary fish without having to dive down deep."

Grand Caico Island is the center of commerce and tourism for the Turks and Caicos, but once you travel to some of the more remote "out" islands, you find small, intimate, locally owned hotels and restaurants interspersed among clusters of private homes. Ben finds this perfect blend of luxury and intimacy on Parrot Cay, which combines the privacy of bungalows on the beach with all the amenities of a world-class hotel.

"I grew up in Boston," says Ben, "which is about as far from the Caribbean mindset, people, and culture as you can find. As a kid in grade school and high school, I became a fanatical lover of Bob Marley. I read all his biographies and decided to go down to the Caribbean to see what this lifestyle and philosophy of life were all about. My first island visit was to Jamaica when I was a senior in high school, and that gave me the appetite to explore other islands. Now, I go to the Caribbean whenever I get a chance. It's as close to heaven as you are ever going to find. At one time, I truly wanted to develop a television series like *Flipper* so that I could spend months at a time there." So tropical, undiscovered, and natural are the island jewels of the Turks and Caicos that Ben posits that the mangoes growing on a tree next to you today "will be served at the restaurant you are dining at tomorrow."

A perfect Caribbean day for Ben is having the luxury of sleeping until 9:00 or 10:00 in the morning, then going for a relaxing swim, enjoying the sun, and feasting on the unique and delicious food served at two of Parrot Cay's very distinctive eating establishments. The Shambhala Spa serves dishes inspired by the philosophy of "life foodists," drawing from ingredients that are seasonal, largely organic, and frequently raw. The Lotus restaurant is renowned for its Asian-fusion cuisine; but according to Ben, it also has the best hamburgers and fries he's ever tasted—not to mention the signature Chocolate Hazelnut Cake.

"This cake is absolutely delicious," Ben raves. "It's pretty simple and straightforward, but the flavors are great. I don't claim to be all that sophisticated when it comes to fine food, but I know what I love when it goes into my mouth, and that Chocolate Hazelnut Cake is really amazing—light and fluffy and full of ground hazelnuts."

Ben also relishes the "pure, simple, and authentic" flavors and tastes found in the smaller restaurants throughout the Caribbean. "These are the places where you can eat like a king for ten dollars," he says. "The conch fritters, mango salsas, rice and beans, and jerk dishes are so good that I can imagine feasting on them right now!

"One of the great things about Caribbean cooking," he continues, "is that it so perfectly combines spiciness and sweetness. The hallmark of almost every recipe down there is that the chefs add an equal amount of each of these taste sensations to every meal."

Shrimp and Raw Green Mango Salad

SHAMBHALA SPA AT PARROT CAY RESORT, CHEF RICHARD THOMPSON

Makes 2 servings (and 1½ cups [360 ml] dressing)

This amazing seafood salad requires only about ¼ cup (60 ml) of dressing, so cut the recipe in half if you don't anticipate a need for a lot of leftovers. Of course, once you taste this delicious, fat-free creation, you may wish you had more on hand.

DRESSING

1 THAI CHILE PEPPER

1 RED FRESNO CHILE PEPPER (SEE NOTE)

½ CUP (120 ML) RAW HONEY

½ CUP (120 ML) APPLE CIDER VINEGAR

½ CUP (120 ML) FRESH LIME JUICE

SALAD

1 RED BELL PEPPER, CORED, SEEDED, AND CUT INTO THIN STRIPS

1 GREEN MANGO, PEELED AND CUT INTO THIN STRIPS

1 ENGLISH CUCUMBER, CUT INTO THIN STRIPS

1 TABLESPOON (15 ML) FRESH GINGER, GRATED

10 MINT LEAVES, CUT INTO THIN STRIPS

2 TABLESPOONS (30 ML) CHOPPED FRESH CILANTRO

¼ CUP (60 ML) CHOPPED RED ONION

¼ CUP (60 ML) DRIED PINEAPPLE, FOR GARNISH

8 EXTRA-LARGE SHRIMP, PEELED AND DEVEINED, POACHED, AND CHILLED

TO MAKE THE DRESSING: Remove and discard the seeds from the chile peppers. In a food processor or blender, chop the chile peppers, then add the honey, vinegar, and lime juice and process until smooth. Set aside. Refrigerate unused amount for up to 1 month.

TO MAKE THE SALAD: In a salad bowl, combine the bell pepper, mango, cucumber, ginger, mint, cilantro, and onion and toss gently with ¼ cup (60 ml) of the dressing. Arrange the salad on 2 plates and garnish with the pineapple. Arrange the shrimp on top.

NOTE: *Wear plastic gloves when handling chile peppers, and wash your hands thoroughly with soap and water before touching sensitive parts of your body, especially your face. To reduce the heat in the finished dish, use only the sides of the pepper (discard seeds and core).*

Chocolate Hazelnut Cake

LOTUS AT THE PARROT CAY RESORT, CHEF RICHARD THOMPSON

Makes 8 servings

¾ CUP (180 ML) UNSALTED BUTTER

¾ CUP (180 ML) GRANULATED SUGAR

5 EGG YOLKS

1¼ CUPS (300 ML) GROUND HAZELNUTS

10 OUNCES (283 G) MELTED DARK CHOCOLATE, COOLED

CONFECTIONERS' SUGAR

Preheat the oven to 300°F (150°C). Grease and flour the bottom of a 9" (23 cm) springform pan.

In an electric mixer fitted with a paddle attachment, cream together the butter and sugar. Add the egg yolks and beat until the mixture lightens in color. Fold in the hazelnuts, then fold in the chocolate. Transfer to the prepared pan and bake for 40 minutes. Let cool in the pan. Release the cake from the pan. Dust with the sugar before serving. Can be made up to 2 days ahead and stored in the refrigerator. Bring to room temperature before serving.

ST. THOMAS

Raven Symone

A LOVE FOR CARIBBEAN CUISINE

Although she's barely out of her teens, Raven Symone has a résumé that would be impressive for a performer twice her age. In fact, she's been captivating audiences since the age of 3, when she was cast as the precocious Olivia Kendall in the *Cosby Show.* When the show went off the air, she moved on without skipping a beat to a 4-year stint in another popular sitcom, *Hangin' with Mr. Cooper.* Currently, she's starring as herself in the Disney Channel's hit series *That's So Raven.*

On the big screen, she has appeared opposite Eddie Murphy in *Dr. Doolittle* and *Dr. Doolittle 2,* in *The Princess Diaries 2: The Royal Engagement,* and most recently, in *All American Girl.*

In addition to being a talented actor, Raven is a gifted singer, who released her third album, *This Is My Time,* in September 2004.

As passionate about food as she is about her work, the young dynamo spends much of her downtime watching Emeril and other celebrity chefs on the Food Network. Her dream is to attend culinary school and then open a restaurant serving a fusion of Caribbean, French, and Southern cuisines.

Ever since she began visiting St. Thomas and other places in the Virgin Islands at a very young age, Raven has been fascinated by what it is that makes island cuisine so tasty and tantalizing. She has learned that this distinctive and enduring style of cooking is based on recipes handed down from generation to generation, and she delights in the various dishes that capture the unique flavors of the region.

"I love the fact that they mix fruits and vegetables with savory fish and meats," says Raven. "Part of their culture is being able to taste the food for what it's meant to be. Most island food isn't doctored up with heavy sauces to make it taste like something it's not. It's a pleasure you have to experience on the islands to understand fully."

In addition to memories of good meals, she fondly recalls relaxing on the beach to work on her tan, sip a Virgin Strawberry Daiquiri, watch all the cute boys walk by, and gaze at the crystal-clear waters of the Caribbean while her parents and younger brother, Blaize, went exploring. "You really get a feeling of being connected to the world when you're in the middle of the ocean or sea and there aren't big areas of land around you," she explains. "When I walked on those beaches, all I saw was the water for miles and miles." Once the family returned, big sister felt obligated to participate in a little sibling roughhousing and even built an occasional sand castle on the beach. But ultimately, the day turned to dining and a good-natured shrimp-eating competition.

Raven doesn't eat beef, so she particularly relished the enormous variety of fresh fish and seafood. "They don't overcook their seafood, so you really feel that you're tasting the ocean through the fish. Seafood that's been sautéed with just a little bit of lime or lemon juice provides a wonderful taste sensation. Then, when it's cooked in a gumbo, you have an entirely different experience. I'm in love with scallops, but they have to be cooked just right—not too chewy and not undercooked. It takes a good chef to cook a scallop!"

Orange roughy is another fish that speaks to Raven's soul. Her own recipe is the closest she's come to true island cooking at home—letting the natural flavor of the fish shine through is what makes this dish so delicious. She buys the roughy as fresh as she can get it and puts the fillets in a glass casserole covered with diced tomatoes, a little salt and pepper, red onion slices, and a drizzle of olive oil, then bakes the fish until just tender and flaky. "Cooking it the way I do," she says, "you're not covering up the taste, you're enhancing it. This dish lets the fish speak for itself."

Her love of food is deeply connected to her family's Southern roots and particularly her grandmother's kitchen. "Her kitchen always smelled so good, and that aroma, coupled with the sight of all that great food, was what brought me to cooking. I'm always in the kitchen, and I've learned how to create something so good from simple elements, such as yams, with just syrup and nutmeg, which can translate into my Sweet Potato Pie." Of the restaurant she hopes to open someday, Raven says, "When I prepare Thanksgiving dinner at home, I serve an Italian pasta dish right along with shrimp and greens and Japanese dumplings, and my restaurant will have that same diversity, from plantains and butter beans to Kalua pork and my favorite orange roughy."

Cajun Gumbo

FROM THE KITCHEN OF RAVEN SYMONE

Makes 8 servings

¾ CUP (180 ML) VEGETABLE OIL

¾ CUP (180 ML) ALL-PURPOSE FLOUR

3 ONIONS, CHOPPED

3 SMALL BELL PEPPERS, ANY COLOR, CORED, SEEDED, AND CHOPPED

4 RIBS CELERY, CHOPPED

6 CLOVES GARLIC, FINELY CHOPPED

8 CUPS (2 L) CHICKEN BROTH OR WATER

1 TABLESPOON (15 ML) CREOLE SEASONING

1 TEASPOON (5 ML) SALT

½ TEASPOON (2.5 ML) FRESHLY GROUND BLACK PEPPER

½ TEASPOON (2.5 ML) CAYENNE PEPPER

1 POUND (454 G) SMOKED SAUSAGE, SLICED (OPTIONAL)

2 POUNDS (1 KG) SHRIMP, PEELED AND DEVEINED, TAILS REMOVED

1 CAN (16 OUNCES [454 G]) CRABMEAT

1 PINT (480 ML) RAW OYSTERS

2 POUNDS (1 KG) CRAWFISH (OPTIONAL)

½ CUP (120 ML) CHOPPED FRESH PARSLEY, FOR GARNISH

½ CUP (120 ML) CHOPPED SCALLIONS, FOR GARNISH

FILÉ POWDER

In a large stockpot over medium-low heat, combine the oil and flour, stirring slowly and constantly until golden brown, about 15 minutes. Add the onions and bell peppers and cook until softened, for 3 to 4 minutes. Add the celery and garlic and cook, stirring, for 5 to 7 minutes. Add the broth, Creole seasoning, salt, pepper, and cayenne. Add the sausage, if using. Bring to a boil, then reduce the heat to low and simmer, covered, for 45 minutes.

Add the shrimp, crabmeat, oysters, and crawfish, if using, and simmer for a few minutes, or until the shrimp turn pink and the edges of the oysters curl. Serve garnished with the parsley and scallions over rice, if desired. Season to taste with the filé powder.

Fresh Orange Roughy

FROM THE KITCHEN OF RAVEN SYMONE

Makes 6 servings

5 ROMA TOMATOES, SLICED

1 ONION OR 5 SHALLOTS, SLICED

2 POUNDS (1 KG) ORANGE ROUGHY FILLETS

SALT AND FRESHLY GROUND BLACK PEPPER

1 TABLESPOON (15 ML) OLIVE OIL

3 TABLESPOONS (45 ML) WATER

Preheat the oven to 350°F (180°C).

Coat the bottom of a 13" x 9" (32.5 x 23 cm) ovenproof baking dish with cooking spray. Spread the tomatoes and onion or shallots in the dish, and lay the fish on top. Season with salt and pepper to taste, and drizzle with the oil to coat the fish. Sprinkle with the water, cover with foil, and bake for about 30 minutes, until the fish flakes easily with a fork.

Raven's Creamy Sweet Potato Pie

FROM THE KITCHEN OF RAVEN SYMONE

Makes 8 servings

1 CAN (16 OUNCES [454 G]) SWEET POTATOES

¾ CUP (180 ML) DARK BROWN SUGAR

1 TEASPOON (5 ML) VANILLA EXTRACT

½ TEASPOON (2.5 ML) SALT

1 TEASPOON (5 ML) GROUND CINNAMON

½ TEASPOON (2.5 ML) GROUND NUTMEG

½ TEASPOON (2.5 ML) GROUND GINGER

¼ TEASPOON (1.2 ML) GROUND CLOVES

2 EGGS, SLIGHTLY BEATEN

1 CAN (12 FLUID OUNCES [360 ML]) EVAPORATED MILK

1 FROZEN DEEP-DISH PIECRUST

WHIPPED CREAM OR REDDI-WIP

In a large bowl, using an electric mixer on medium speed, beat the sweet potatoes until smooth and set aside. Mix in the brown sugar, vanilla extract, salt, cinnamon, nutmeg, ginger, and cloves, stirring until well blended. Stir in the eggs and milk until well blended. Pour into the crust and bake for 55 to 60 minutes. Just before serving, top with whipped cream.

Raven's Virgin Strawberry Daiquiris

FROM THE KITCHEN OF RAVEN SYMONE

Makes 6 servings

3 CUPS (720 ML) SLICED FRESH STRAWBERRIES (FROZEN CAN BE USED, IF NECESSARY)

¼ CUP (60 ML) FRESH LIME JUICE

1 CAN (12 FLUID OUNCES [360 ML]) LIMEADE CONCENTRATE

3 CUPS (720 ML) WATER OR JUICE (CRANBERRY, STRAWBERRY, ETC.) OF YOUR CHOICE

1 CUP (240 ML) ICE

LIME SLICES AND STRAWBERRIES, FOR GARNISH

In a blender, combine the strawberries, lime juice, limeade concentrate, and water or juice and process until smooth. Add the ice and process until the mixture reaches the desired consistency. Serve immediately, garnished with the limes and strawberries.

VIRGIN GORDA

Morgan Freeman

IT'S A SAILOR'S LIFE FOR ME

Morgan Freeman hit acting gold when he won both an Oscar and a Golden Globe for his remarkable performance in *Million Dollar Baby* in 2004. Prior to that "winningest" year, however, he had already received three Academy Award nominations—for *Street Smart, Driving Miss Daisy,* and *The Shawshank Redemption*—and won a Golden Globe for *Driving Miss Daisy.* A few of Morgan's other outstanding films include *Glory, Se7en,* and *Amistad.* In addition, he forever defined the role of Detective Alex Cross in *Kiss the Girls* and *Along Came a Spider* and appeared opposite Jim Carrey in the 2003 smash hit *Bruce Almighty,* playing—who else?—God.

Ever since he first sailed to the Caribbean in 1989, Morgan has spent as much time as possible exploring the islands. When he visits Virgin Gorda, where he is currently building a home, he docks his boat near Little Dix Bay.

"There is a real sense of freedom when I sail, especially alone in deep waters," says Morgan, "that must be similar to flying." It was his love of sailing, in fact, that led him to discover the Caribbean islands, where he fell in love once more. There is a feeling of warmth, a sense of tranquility, and an openness about the islands and their people that Morgan always looks forward to revisiting after months of filming in the States.

That straightforward simplicity is reflected in the food of the Caribbean, and that, too, suits Morgan very well. "I like to eat, but I don't live to eat—I'm a strange bird that way. And when I'm on the islands, I like basic foods. I like to eat what the local people eat, and that includes fish such as conch fritters and grouper with rice. I also love dishes cooked with pineapple and coconut. One of my favorite foods down there is sushi made with tuna that has literally just been snatched from the sea. Frequently, my wife, Myrna, and I also eat on the boat, where she is the cook—certainly not me!"

When he's docked at Virgin Gorda and in the mood for something a little more elaborate, Morgan visits the Bath & Turtle or Chez Bamboo, both owned by Rose Giacinto.

"Morgan loves fresh fish just slightly grilled, the fresher the better," says Rose. "It's all about the sauces, and his favorites include a lemon-caperberry butter sauce as well as the more traditional teriyaki sauce. He also loves our jerk chicken salad on a bed of baby greens with a honey-lime, Caribbean-style vinaigrette that's both a little bit sweet and slightly peppery.

"Then, of course, there are the Tamarind-Ginger Chicken Wings, a popular specialty from Chez Bamboo that Morgan loves to snack on. He and Myrna will come into the restaurant in the later afternoon and sit over at the pub having a piña colada and wings, and that will be their dinner. The woman who created the sauce for our wings is from Grenada." When Morgan is hosting a large gathering, Rose says, he always wants a taste of what everyone else is eating. One of the reasons he keeps returning to the islands, she believes, is that "although everyone knows he's a big movie star, he is also a very simple man in his heart and soul, and that's the way he's treated around here."

BATH & TURTLE RESTAURANT

Spanish Town, Virgin Gorda

Owner Rose Giacinto

The very "happening" and always busy Bath & Turtle is located in the center of the Virgin Gorda Yacht Harbor, where it acts as a kind of local living room for the sailors docked there. Open every day of the year, its success is based upon serving a diverse and delicious menu in a welcoming and casual atmosphere.

Many Bath & Turtle diners have their main meals in the middle of the day, and owner Rose Giacinto accommodates them by serving a variety of homemade soups that are often as hearty as

stews. "Our chicken soup," she says, "is full of bite-size pieces of chicken, potatoes, green plantain, and sweet potato, as well as local tannia and dasheen, both of which are similar to potatoes; all the vegetables that thicken the soup are grown in the ground. We also add fresh thyme, carrots, celery, and homemade dumplings.

"I truly have a very diverse island staff, including people from St. Kitts, Grenada, St. Lucia, St. Maarten, and Santo Domingo, and our cuisine reflects this down-island mix," says Rose, who grew up in the United States and moved to the tiny island of Marina Key when she got married. In 1987, the Bath & Turtle became available, and the Giacintos purchased it. When her husband passed away, Rose decided to carry on alone, and Morgan and Myrna, along with thousands of other faithful diners, are very glad she did.

Local Chicken Soup

BATH & TURTLE, OWNER ROSE GIACINTO

Makes 8 servings

DUMPLINGS

¾ CUP (180 ML) ALL-PURPOSE FLOUR

1 TABLESPOON (15 ML) CORNMEAL

1½ TEASPOONS (7.5 ML) BAKING POWDER

1 TEASPOON (5 ML) SUGAR

½ TEASPOON (2.5 ML) SALT

1 TABLESPOON (15 ML) BUTTER

½ CUP (120 ML) FAT-FREE MILK

SOUP

1 WHOLE CHICKEN, ABOUT 4 POUNDS (1.8 KG)

1 PACKET COCK SOUP OR DRY CHICKEN SOUP MIX

1 TABLESPOON (15 ML) GOYA SAZON WITH ANNATTO

2 CLOVES GARLIC, MINCED

3 SPRIGS FRESH THYME

1 BUNCH SCALLIONS

2 BAY LEAVES

2 RIBS CELERY

1 MEDIUM ONION

4 MEDIUM ALL-PURPOSE POTATOES

3 MEDIUM CARROTS

2 GREEN PLANTAINS

2 SWEET POTATOES

2 SWEET YAMS

1 TANNIA (SEE RESOURCES, PAGE 247)

½ POUND (227 G) CABOCHA OR BUTTERNUT SQUASH

1 SCOTCH BONNET OR HABANERO CHILE PEPPER

TO MAKE THE DUMPLINGS: In a large bowl, combine the flour, cornmeal, baking powder, sugar, and salt. Use a pastry cutter to cut the butter into the mixture, until the dough is the texture of coarse meal. Add the milk and stir just until moist. Form into small balls and set aside.

TO MAKE THE SOUP: Cut up the chicken, separating the legs from the thighs, removing the wings from the breast, and cutting the breast into 4 pieces (10 pieces in all; remove the skin if you prefer a leaner dish).

Place the chicken, soup mix, sazon, and garlic in a large stockpot and add enough cold water to cover the chicken completely. With butcher's twine, tie the thyme, scallions, bay leaves, and celery into a bundle. Add to the pot and bring to a boil over high heat, then reduce the heat and simmer for about 15 minutes.

Peel and dice the onion, potatoes, carrots, plantains, sweet potatoes, yams, tannia, and squash. Add to the pot and increase the heat. When the soup boils, add the dumplings. Drop in the chile pepper. Reduce the heat and simmer until the vegetables are tender. Remove the herb bundle just before serving

Caribbean Chicken Salad with Lime Vinaigrette

BATH & TURTLE, OWNER ROSE GIACINTO

Rose serves this spicy chicken salad—one of the Freemans' lunchtime favorites—with a sweet, tangy dressing that's equally delicious on a simple mixed-green salad.

Makes 4 servings (1⅔ cups [320 ml] dressing)

DRESSING

½ RED BELL PEPPER, CORED, SEEDED, AND CHOPPED

½ GREEN BELL PEPPER, CORED, SEEDED, AND CHOPPED

1 CLOVE GARLIC

¼ CUP (60 ML) HONEY

¼ CUP (60 ML) KEY LIME JUICE

½ CUP (120 ML) OLIVE OIL

2 TABLESPOONS (30 ML) DISTILLED WHITE VINEGAR

½ TEASPOON (2.5 ML) DIJON MUSTARD

SALAD

1 POUND (454 G) BONELESS, SKINLESS CHICKEN BREAST HALVES

¼ CUP (60 ML) JERK SEASONING

8 CUPS (2 L) MIXED BABY GREENS

1 CUP (240 ML) THINLY SLICED RED CABBAGE

½ RED BELL PEPPER, CORED, SEEDED, AND SLICED

½ GREEN BELL PEPPER, CORED, SEEDED, AND SLICED

½ RED ONION, SLICED

4 HARD-COOKED EGGS, QUARTERED

TO MAKE THE DRESSING: In a food processor, combine the peppers and garlic and process with on/off pulses until chopped. Add the honey, lime juice, oil, vinegar, and mustard and blend until smooth. You can make the dressing ahead and store in an airtight container for up to 3 days.

TO MAKE THE SALAD: In a resealable plastic bag, combine the chicken and jerk seasoning and refrigerate for at least 1 hour or preferably overnight.

Preheat the grill to high. Grill the chicken for 4 to 5 minutes per side, until it's no longer pink inside and the juices run clear. Transfer to a plate and set aside.

Arrange equal portions of the greens on 4 large salad plates, and top with equal portions of the cabbage, bell peppers, and onion. Slice the chicken into thin strips and divide equally among the plates. Top with the eggs and serve with the dressing on the side.

Curry Chicken Kebabs

BATH & TURTLE, OWNER ROSE GIACINTO

Makes 2 servings

3 TABLESPOONS (45 ML) RED CURRY PASTE

½ CUP (120 ML) COCONUT MILK

JUICE OF 1 LIME

1 TABLESPOON (15 ML) EXTRA-VIRGIN OLIVE OIL

SEA SALT AND FRESHLY GROUND BLACK PEPPER

2 BONELESS, SKINLESS CHICKEN BREASTS, EACH CUT LENGTHWISE INTO 4 PIECES

1 RED, GREEN, OR YELLOW BELL PEPPER, CORED, SEEDED, AND CHOPPED INTO 16 PIECES

1 LARGE YELLOW ONION, CHOPPED INTO 16 PIECES

In a medium bowl, combine the curry paste, coconut milk, lime juice, oil, and salt and pepper to taste. Add the chicken and turn to coat well. Cover and refrigerate for at least 2 hours or overnight.

Preheat the grill and soak 4 bamboo skewers in water for 20 minutes. Divide the chicken and vegetables equally among the skewers, and grill for 2 to 3 minutes on each side, until chicken is no longer pink inside.

Conch Quesadillas

BATH & TURTLE, OWNER ROSE GIACINTO

Makes 4 servings

- 2 TABLESPOONS (30 ML) OLIVE OIL
- 1 SMALL ONION, DICED
- 1 RED BELL PEPPER, CORED, SEEDED, AND DICED
- 1 GREEN BELL PEPPER, CORED, SEEDED, AND DICED
- 2 JALAPEÑO CHILE PEPPERS, SEEDED AND DICED + ADDITIONAL FOR GARNISH (SEE NOTE)

- 2 CUPS (480 ML) GROUND CONCH MEAT OR CLAMS
- 2 EGGS, BEATEN
- 1 TEASPOON (5 ML) ALL-PURPOSE FLOUR
- 8 (8" [20 CM]) FLOUR TORTILLAS
- 8 TABLESPOONS (120 ML) CREAM CHEESE, SOFTENED

Preheat the oven to 425°F (220°C).

Heat the oil in a medium skillet over medium heat. Add the onion, bell peppers, and jalapeños and sauté until the onion sweats. Add the conch, eggs, and flour, stir, and sauté for 2 minutes. Spread ¼ of the mixture on 1 tortilla, top with another tortilla, and press to flatten. Place in a large nonstick skillet and cook for about 2 minutes per side, or until lightly browned. Transfer to a baking sheet large enough to hold all the tortillas, top with a dollop of cream cheese, and sprinkle with diced jalapeño. Repeat with the remaining tortillas and filling. Bake for 5 minutes, then cut each quesadilla into 4 triangles.

NOTE: *Wear plastic gloves when handling chile peppers, and wash your hands thoroughly with soap and water before touching sensitive parts of your body, especially your face. To reduce the heat in the finished dish, use only the sides of the pepper (discard seeds and core).*

Grilled Swordfish Steak
with Lemon-Caperberry Butter Sauce

CHEZ BAMBOO, OWNER ROSE GIACINTO

Makes 4 servings

SWORDFISH

4 TEASPOONS (20 ML) MINCED GARLIC

1 TEASPOON (5 ML) CURRY POWDER

2 TABLESPOONS (60 ML) OLIVE OIL

SALT AND FRESHLY GROUND BLACK PEPPER

4 (6 OUNCES [170 G] EACH) SWORDFISH STEAKS,
   1" (2.5 CM) THICK

SAUCE

1 TEASPOON (5 ML) BUTTER

3 SHALLOTS, MINCED

1 TABLESPOON (15 ML) BRANDY

6 TABLESPOONS (90 ML) FISH STOCK

4 TABLESPOONS (60 ML) WHITE WINE

2 TABLESPOONS (30 ML) FRESH LEMON JUICE

4 TABLESPOONS (60 ML) CHOPPED CAPERBERRIES

½ CUP (120 ML) HEAVY CREAM

TO PREPARE THE FISH: In a baking dish large enough to hold the fish in a single layer, combine the garlic, curry powder, oil, and salt and pepper to taste. Add the fish, turning to coat on both sides, and refrigerate for 1 hour.

TO MAKE THE SAUCE: Melt the butter in a medium skillet over medium heat. Add the shallots and sauté until soft, about 2 minutes. Add the brandy, stock, and wine and sauté until slightly thickened, about 3 minutes. Add the lemon juice and caperberries and simmer for 2 to 3 minutes to allow the flavors to combine. Add the heavy cream and cook 2 minutes longer, until warmed through.

Preheat the grill to high. Grill the fish for 4 minutes on each side. Transfer to 4 plates, and spoon the sauce over the fish.

Lobster Curry

CHEZ BAMBOO, OWNER ROSE GIACINTO

This creamy curry is delicious with a side of garlic mashed potatoes.

Makes 4 servings

1 POUND (454 G) LOBSTER MEAT, CUT INTO 2"
   (5 CM) PIECES

¼ CUP (60 ML) ALL-PURPOSE FLOUR

2 TABLESPOONS (30 ML) OIL

2 CLOVES GARLIC, MINCED

½ CUP (120 ML) WHITE WINE

2 TABLESPOONS (30 ML) CURRY POWDER

2 CUPS (480 ML) HEAVY CREAM

½ CUP (120 ML) COCONUT CREAM

SALT AND FRESHLY GROUND BLACK PEPPER

Dust the lobster with the flour. Heat the oil in a large skillet over medium heat. Add the lobster and sauté until opaque and cooked through. Transfer to a plate.

Add the garlic, wine, and curry powder to the skillet and cook until reduced by half. Add the heavy cream and coconut cream and simmer for 4 minutes. Return the lobster to the skillet and heat until warmed through. Season to taste with the salt and pepper and serve immediately.

Rose's Cappuccino Cheesecake

CHEZ BAMBOO, OWNER ROSE GIACINTO

Makes 8 servings

CRUST

8 GRAHAM CRACKERS (ABOUT 1 CUP [240 ML] +
2 TABLESPOONS [30 ML] CRUMBS)

¼ CUP (60 ML) SUGAR

5 TABLESPOONS (75 ML) UNSALTED BUTTER,
MELTED

1 TEASPOON (5 ML) ESPRESSO POWDER

1 TEASPOON (5 ML) COCOA POWDER

FILLING

2 PACKAGES (8 OUNCES [227 G] EACH) CREAM
CHEESE, AT ROOM TEMPERATURE

½ CUP (120 ML) DARK BROWN SUGAR

⅓ CUP (80 ML) GRANULATED SUGAR

1½ TEASPOONS (7.5 ML) ESPRESSO POWDER

2 EGG YOLKS

1 TEASPOON (5 ML) KAHLUA

WHIPPED CREAM

COCOA POWDER

Preheat the oven to 325°F (160°C). Wrap the outside of a 7" or 8" (18 cm or 20 cm) springform pan with foil.

TO MAKE THE CRUST: In a food processor, combine the graham crackers, sugar, butter, espresso powder, and cocoa powder and process until crumbly. Press the crumbs into the bottom of the prepared pan.

TO MAKE THE FILLING: After rinsing the bowl and blades of the food processor, add the cream cheese, brown sugar, granulated sugar, espresso powder, egg yolks, and Kahlua and process until smooth. Pour into the crust. Pour ½" (1.25 cm) of water into a roasting pan and place the cheesecake pan in the water bath. Bake for 40 to 50 minutes, or until the filling is firm. Remove from the water bath and let cool to room temperature, then refrigerate overnight. Remove from the refrigerator 20 minutes before serving, and release the cheesecake from the pan. Top each serving with a dollop of whipped cream and a sprinkling of cocoa powder.

ST. JOHN

Kenny Chesney

POSTCARDS FROM ST. JOHN

The hits just keep coming for Kenny Chesney, who was named both the Country Music Association's and the Academy of Country Music's Entertainer of the Year in 2004 and *People* magazine's Sexiest Country Singer Alive in 2005. The past few years have been very good and very prolific for him. *When the Sun Goes Down; No Shoes, No Shirt, No Problems;* and *Greatest Hits* passed quadruple platinum and continue to inch toward the 5,000,000 mark. In 2004, he was also named Artist of the Year at the American Music Awards. In 2005, he won the Triple Crown Award at the Country Music Awards.

Now multiplatinum, *Be As You Are* is an album of what Kenny calls postcards to and about the people he's met and the things he's experienced during the decade he has been visiting the Caribbean.

Although he's moved on to new challenges and released *The Road and the Radio* in late fall 2005, Kenny still carries the island spirit with him every day.

One of the most successful country music stars in the world today, Kenny started visiting St. John more than 10 years ago, when his career was just beginning to take off. He arrived the day before Christmas Eve to shoot a music video and stayed only 36 hours, but that was long enough for him to fall in love with the island lifestyle. In fact, he returned just a few weeks later.

"After hanging out for a few days, I started to meet some great people who were to become life-long friends," says Kenny. "I fell in love with the people, the way they live their lives, and the way they make me feel. When I'm out on the road, I'm a very focused person; I always have a deadline and a place that I have to be. But when I'm on St. John, my life doesn't revolve around schedules, and I don't have to meet expectations. I can go out on my boat and just watch the sun travel across the sky.

"As I began spending more and more time on the island, I tried to learn how not to push so hard. I have a West Indian friend down there who, I swear, has never worn a pair of shoes in his whole life. He either goes barefoot or wears flip-flops. I try to take some of that feeling out on the road with me now, and I even take my crew down there after our tour is over, because I want them to experience the lifestyle and understand why it's so important to me."

It was only a matter of time before his love for the Caribbean started to make its way into his music. For years, after a tour finished, Kenny would spend several months there on his boat, unwinding, relaxing, and recharging his emotional batteries. One of the ways he recentered himself was to keep a journal, which soon grew into several books jam-packed with reflections and song ideas. When staying at small beachside campsites, he met people from other countries and listened to their stories.

"I started writing songs about the people I met and how they lived their lives," he explains. "The songs on *Be As You Are: Songs from an Old Blue Chair* are really those stories set to music. At the time, I didn't know these musical reflections were going to turn into an album; I had just planned to play the songs for the people they were written about. The album is like a bunch of postcards, snapshots of the people I've met during my island travels."

In fact, the album's title comes from the old blue rocking chair that came with the house he rented when he first began visiting St. John. "I'd just sit in that chair and rock for hours," he recalls, "doing a lot of soul-searching.

"I let go emotionally of somebody in that chair and that New Year's Eve had way too much to drink, rolled up my pant legs, and went down to sit in that chair on the beach, with a rum drink between my legs, and fell asleep," remembers Kenny. "The next morning, I woke up with the sun rising over Tortola, and I was still in that chair, but unfortunately had some unexpected company and just as my song says, 'I woke up with a hundred mosquito bites there. . . .' But I realized that morning that I had to make myself happy, and that is why I have such an emotional attachment to that chair.

"Once we decided to release that album, I was a little worried about whether my fans who had never visited the Caribbean would be able to relate to it. Then I thought, 'I'm gonna take them there through this record and paint some pictures for them through the words and music.' *Be As You Are* ultimately turned out to be one of the most satisfying things I've ever done professionally."

Personally, one of the things that satisfies Kenny most is a great big slice of key lime pie, which, he says, has been his favorite dessert "forever." When he's on the road, his strenuous tour regimen includes daily workouts with a trainer, and there's little room for indulgent desserts. On St. John, however, it's one of the many delights of his downtime. So great is his passion, in fact, that he immortalized the dessert in one of the most popular songs on his *Be As You Are* album, entitled (what else?) "Key Lime Pie."

Kenny's friend Jerome, who owns a restaurant on St. John and makes the "best key lime pie on the island," has shared the recipe with him. According to Kenny and Jerome, the key to the recipe's success is using lots of fresh lime juice—the more juice, the more flavorful the pie!

"Many of my friends there on St. John own or work in the local restaurants," explains Kenny. "When you live on an island, you are one of the four Bs—a boatie, bartender, builder, or bum—and most of my friends fit into at least one of those categories. Because I'm so strict about my diet during most of the year, when I'm down there, I eat everything from a big fat cheeseburger and jerk chicken to lots of mango sauces and, of course, key lime pie. I love fresh fruit, and I have mango and banana trees in my front yard. I just love being able to pick my own fresh fruit whenever I want to. When I'm living on the boat, of course, it's definitely back to basics with simple grilled salmon, chicken, or turkey."

Having finally arrived at a place where he feels comfortable both personally and professionally exploring the things that make him happy, Kenny loves putting on a cowboy hat and an old pair of flip-flops and being called an island cowboy.

Kenny Chesney's Favorite Key Lime Pie

Makes 8 servings

CRUST

1¼ CUPS (300 ML) GRAHAM CRACKER CRUMBS

¼ CUP (60 ML) SUGAR

5 TABLESPOONS (75 ML) UNSALTED BUTTER, MELTED

TOPPING

1 CONTAINER (8 OUNCES [227 G]) WHIPPED TOPPING, THAWED

LIME SLICES

FILLING

4 EGG YOLKS

1 CAN (14 FLUID OUNCES [420 ML]) SWEETENED CONDENSED MILK

½ CUP (120 ML) FRESH LIME JUICE (2–3 LIMES)

2 TEASPOONS (10 ML) GRATED LIME ZEST

TO MAKE THE CRUST: Preheat the oven to 325°F (160°C).

In a medium bowl, combine the graham cracker crumbs and sugar. Add the butter, stir with a fork until blended, and transfer to a 9" (23 cm) deep-dish pie pan. Press the crumbs with your fingers onto the sides and then the bottom of the pan, then press again with the bottom of a measuring cup to ensure a firm crust. Bake on the center oven rack for about 15 minutes, or until golden brown. Let cool to room temperature.

TO MAKE THE FILLING: Place the egg yolks, milk, lime juice, and lime zest in a medium bowl. Using an electric mixer on high speed, beat for about 3 minutes, or until thick.

When the crust is cool, pour in the filling and spread it evenly. Bake for 15 minutes, or until the center is set but still jiggles when shaken. Let cool to room temperature, then cover with the whipped topping and garnish with the lime slices. Refrigerate for at least 3 hours, or until well chilled.

ST. CROIX

Tim Robbins

REDEMPTION FOUND

St. Croix holds special memories for Morgan Freeman and his fellow actor and dear friend Tim Robbins, as it's where they filmed the final scene of *The Shawshank Redemption,* the 1994 movie that was nominated for seven Academy Awards and is widely regarded as one of the greatest films of all time. In the movie, Tim and Morgan's characters reconnect on a beautiful beach on the island after forging an unlikely friendship while serving hard time in prison. Off the screen, more than a decade later, Morgan and Tim met in Los Angeles (Tim was in town to perform with his famed theater group, The Actors' Gang, for a homeless shelter and services benefit—an event whose all-star cast included Morgan) to enjoy good Caribbean food and reminisce about St. Croix and other island memories.

When Tim agreed to participate in this book project to benefit Grenada, Morgan said, "Well, if we do this interview together, we'll probably get hungry . . . ," and thought

of the Four Seasons Hotel in Beverly Hills. The Four Seasons holds a special place in Morgan's heart. For more than 2 decades, he's stayed at the resort chain's Los Angeles property exclusively when in LA. The Four Seasons is exceptionally service oriented, and it seems that they can never say no, particularly to Morgan. So when Morgan suggested meeting Tim for dinner at the Seasons, the hotel—with its usual flair—graciously provided a poolside locale for the reunion. Executive Chef Conny Andersson, formerly of the Four Seasons and currently at the Regent Beverly Wilshire, stepped in to create a carnival of sumptuous Caribbean dishes.

Over the course of his career, Conny has traveled to India, Bali, and Europe, but his heart and his palate remain firmly rooted in the Caribbean. He was delighted to prepare a splendid feast and share some hard-earned knowledge about Caribbean delicacies while Tim and Morgan dined beneath the palms that swayed in the September breeze.

The wind was brisk, but plenty of good wine, good food, and conversation about Caribbean times kept spirits warm and high on the autumn afternoon when Conny prepared a scrumptious, four-course meal.

The menu (see page 112 for recipes) was a sophisticated mix of tropical flavors, starting with a lime-fragrant sampler of ackee and salt fish served with johnnycakes, conch two ways (chowder and fritters), and tuna tartare with avocado salsa and pawpaw (aka papaya) salad, all of which the old friends sailed through at top speed as they reminisced.

"When we were shooting the final scene of *The Shawshank Redemption* on the beach in St. Croix, I had my boat moored down there, so I got to live on it for a while. That was heaven," Morgan recalled as he sampled the selections in front of him, starting with Pawpaw Salad.

"Conny, what *is* pawpaw?" asked Tim.

"The word is actually a colloquialism for *papaya*," Conny replied. "This slaw is made from green papaya, which can be done up a lot of different ways in the islands of the Caribbean, but this way is one of my favorites. Go ahead, try it."

Tim complied, and sighs of delight followed.

"I love papaya," chimed in Morgan, having just taken a mouthful of the pawpaw. "It's so good for your digestion. I was in Trinidad once with friends who were rebuilding a boat, and iguanas would come out and wait for us to toss them the rinds of the papaya we were having for breakfast. They loved the stuff, too."

"I took my boys down there, remember?" Tim said, reflecting back on the *Shawshank* shoot. "The oldest one, Jack, got hit by a wave—hard—and he still remembers." Returning his attention to the food, he put another forkful of the salad into his mouth and exclaimed, "Conny, this is delicious. What makes it hot?"

"Habanero chile. You have to be very careful when you're working with it so as not to get the oil in your eyes," the chef explained.

"Well, I grew up in one of those houses where you had to clean your plate—plus, the faster you

ate, the more likely you were to get seconds," claimed Tim as he reached for a johnnycake, wondering aloud where that name came from.

Conny explained: "Johnnycakes are lard biscuits, usually fried, and they're offered in numerous versions throughout the Caribbean." According to Caribbean myth, the name is derived from *journey cake*—bread that was suitable for taking on a journey.

"Well, I learn something every day. That's why I enjoy living," Tim sighed with a mixture of intellectual and gastronomic gratification.

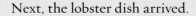

Next, the lobster dish arrived.

"Conny—what have you done? It's just beautiful," Morgan trumpeted when the waiter presented the lobster.

"You know," he continued, "when I got my first big boat, my wife and I would sail up in Maine, and we would make these point-to-point trips. The first time we were headed east from there, they told us, 'You've got to stop in Boothbay and go to Beale's for lobster.' My wife loves lobster. If it starts with an *L* and ends with an *R*, she'll eat it."

"I think one of my boys was conceived after a lobster dinner," Tim added as they dug in.

By the time main courses arrived—the snapper roasted in a banana leaf with mango–black bean relish and the savory, juicy jerk lamb chops—the gentlemen were finishing their first bottle of Sauvignon Blanc and considering a second.

"Sauvignon Blanc is a perfect wine for these dishes," said Conny. "And this one is so crisp and bright, it really levels out the spices. It's almost cleansing."

By then, the island flavors were calling forth more and more Caribbean memories.

"We've been to St. John, the Bahamas, and Parrot Cay," Tim reminisced. "I'm kind of a workaholic—it's more my wife [as he refers to actress Susan Sarandon] who got me down there. We first went to Anguilla when Jack was 1½, and he fell in love with this little girl named Emily who was about 9½. He would say her name over and over again. We've had some great times down there with the kids.

"I took my son Miles on vacation to Turks and Caicos. We were at this really nice resort. On the main island, there was this rink. Miles and I went down and played ice hockey—in the Caribbean! I loved that. The waters there are so shallow that the [big] boats can't go through there. So the water is really clean. I really love swimming in those waters.

"And when you stumble into a festival in a village, that's nice," he continued. "Last year, we were down for Carnival. We had to get the kids up at 3 o'clock in the morning for it. You head over and there's dancing—this great vibe. It's just great."

"There are times when I'm on Virgin Gorda that the island is really jumping," Morgan added as they finished off the main course. "I have a friend there who has a couple of restaurants. On Wednesday and Thursday nights, they have 'jump-ups.' Boy, that's some fun."

"If you're smart, you find the local restaurants, and that's where you get the real flavors of the Caribbean," Tim agreed. "You're not going to discover the culture of the Caribbean in a resort. You have to be an active participant to get what's real. We love that. We've had great meals just wandering down the beach and finding a little place that's cooking up something."

As the sun sank below the LA horizon, the chef brought out the downright risqué finale: plump, golden brown banana beignets with vanilla bean ice cream, swathed in translucent veils of pineapple carpaccio. Morgan was beside himself and raised a fork to meet the dish midair.

Tim's thoughts returned once more to the time he and Morgan spent together on St. Croix. "At the end of the shoot for *Shawshank,* we were dog tired. Going down to the islands was a kind of poetic way to end it. I only wish that you'd taken me sailing, Morgan. But I had my kids with me, and we couldn't.

"I grew up in New York City. I knew how to take the subway—but I never learned much about the water. And I'd like to. I want to learn how to sail. Morgan, I'll be down for my sailing lesson soon."

"Come on down," Morgan retorted as they lifted their nearly empty wineglasses in a toast to the chef and to their dream of sailing off into the sunset. On this day, however, they were content to walk it, full of good wine, amazing food, and happy memories.

THE REGENT BEVERLY WILSHIRE,
A FOUR SEASONS HOTEL

Beverly Hills, California

Conny Andersson, Executive Chef

Caribbean food styles are among Executive Chef Conny Andersson's favorite specialties. After more than 20 years of travel and training, it all comes back to the Caribbean, a place he visits many times a year and where he says his heart will always be, in part because so many ethnic influences converge in island cuisine.

"Foremost in Caribbean food is the African influence—the ackee and breadfruit, jackfruit—all of the plants that were brought with the slaves from Africa. The salted fish that was necessary for travel in the slave triangle mixed with the simple, fresh food preparations of the Caribs and their seafood and vegetables were enhanced by the most natural salts and seasoning elements. When the slave trade was abolished, laborers were sought from China and India. South of Trinidad, there is more of an East Indian influence, and in Jamaica you have a huge Chinese influence—it's surprising, but you'll always see a stir-fry in Jamaica," he explains.

On a recent trip, Conny indulged in a bit of research that is his trademark when traveling. "I always like to learn what people are eating on the streets—this time it was rotis. The Roti King was a shack in St. John's—they probably sell the best rotis north of Trinidad. They were so good, I just couldn't stop eating them.

"Coming from St. Lucia, however, I was still searching for the island *savoir faire*. A cab driver took us out to a beach with a restaurant row. We went to one place where the food was so un-island-like, we left promptly. Then we happened upon a spot on the beach where some people were having a barbecue. In St. Lucia, they're famous for salt fish and green bananas. We had a green banana salad, smothered pork, breadfruit, barbecued chicken, and roti. All of the locals were there. You could tell it was the right place to be—and at the right time."

A recent craze among foodies and seasoned chefs alike are gourmet cruises—sea ventures that feature one or more celebrated chefs supervising seafaring culinary crews as they prepare the chef's

specialties and other dishes developed especially for the journey. These luxurious sojourns have provided more opportunities for Conny to get to his beloved Caribbean.

"Celebrated chefs like Wolfgang Puck and Anton Mosimann are invited to go on the Crystal Cruises line ships, which are like Four Seasons properties on water. I was invited to chef on one of them. These are top-notch vacation cruise experiences—with butlers on station in the luxury cabins (which is where the chefs retire to!). On this particular cruise, we stopped in St. Barth's, St. Maarten, Antigua, St. Lucia, the Panama Canal, and Costa Rica."

Conny continues, "Naturally, the guests are inspired to try foods that feature island flavors when they're sailing in the Caribbean. They want to have something that is unique and reflective of where they are. So, of course, you do a lot of fish. The galley on a ship like that gleams like a star; the chrome shines like the sun. The crews are tight and focused—they have to be to prepare haute cuisine for so many guests with no sacrifice in presentation or quality levels. Guest chefs start with a meeting with the culinary crew and go step-by-step through the planned menu. You do the presentation to make sure everything is the way it should be—you're leaving your reputation in the hands of others. There are a lot of people eating, and you're gonna be on the boat for a week after the main presentation. You want them to love it—close quarters, you know. So you really had better have thought it through. Then you can walk the tables and socialize with the passengers confidently, no?

"It's quite thrilling to have 800 people—a truly captive audience—waiting for you. When it's showtime and it all goes right, those are the moments we live for."

Jerk Lamb Chops with Two Kinds of Plantain, Red Beans, and Coconut Rice, with Tamarind Glaze

CHEF CONNY ANDERSSON

Makes 4 servings

8 DOUBLE-RIB LAMB CHOPS

½ CUP (120 ML) JERK MARINADE
(RECIPE FOLLOWS)

2 CLOVES GARLIC

½ CUP (120 ML) OLIVE OIL

VEGETABLE OIL, FOR FRYING

1 RIPE PLANTAIN, PEELED AND CUT INTO
½" (1.25 CM)-THICK ROUNDS

1 UNRIPE PLANTAIN, PEELED AND CUT INTO
½" (1.25 CM)-THICK ROUNDS

SALT

¼ CUP (60 ML) TAMARIND GLAZE
(RECIPE FOLLOWS)

4 CUPS (1 L) RED BEANS AND COCONUT RICE
(RECIPE FOLLOWS)

In a large bowl, toss the lamb chops in the marinade and refrigerate for 2 hours.

Smash the garlic with the flat side of a chef's knife. Place into a small bowl with the olive oil and set aside to steep.

Meanwhile, heat at least 2" (5 cm) of oil in a large pot over medium-high heat to 360°F (182°C). Working in batches, gently slip the plantains into the oil and fry until golden brown. Transfer to a rack and let cool to room temperature. Flatten with a spatula or the flat side of a chef's knife, then add to the fryer in batches and fry until crisp. Drizzle lightly with a small quantity of the garlic oil, and sprinkle with salt to taste.

Preheat the grill. Remove the chops from the marinade and grill for 4 to 5 minutes on each side, or until a thermometer inserted in the center registers 145°F (63°C) for medium-rare.

To assemble the dish, streak each plate with the glaze, arrange 2 chops on top of the glaze, and surround with the plantains and beans and rice.

JERK MARINADE

Makes 2 cups (480 ml)

½ CUP (120 ML) MINCED SCALLIONS

1 TABLESPOON (15 ML) CHOPPED GARLIC

½ TABLESPOON (7.5 ML) DRIED THYME

¼ CUP (60 ML) DARK BROWN SUGAR

½ TABLESPOON (7.5 ML) GROUND ALLSPICE

½ TABLESPOON (7.5 ML) GROUND CINNAMON

¼ TABLESPOON (1.2 ML) GROUND NUTMEG

1 CUP (240 ML) KETCHUP

½ CUP (120 ML) VEGETABLE OIL

½ CUP (120 ML) CIDER VINEGAR

2 SCOTCH BONNET CHILE PEPPERS, COARSELY CHOPPED (SEE NOTE)

SALT AND FRESHLY GROUND BLACK PEPPER

In a food processor, combine the scallions, garlic, thyme, brown sugar, allspice, cinnamon, nutmeg, ketchup, oil, vinegar, and chile peppers and process until smooth. Season to taste with the salt and pepper.

NOTE: *Wear plastic gloves when handling Scotch bonnet chiles, and wash your hands thoroughly with soap and water before touching sensitive parts of your body, especially your face. To reduce the heat in the finished dish, use only the sides of the pepper (discard the seeds and core).*

(CONTINUED)

TAMARIND GLAZE

Makes 1 cup (240 ml)

1½ TABLESPOONS (22.5 ML) TAMARIND
    CONCENTRATE (SEE RESOURCES, PAGE 247)

1 TABLESPOON (15 ML) VEGETABLE OIL

2 SHALLOTS, FINELY DICED

½ CUP (120 ML) DARK RUM

½ CUP (120 ML) DISTILLED WHITE VINEGAR

½ CUP (120 ML) BROWN SUGAR

½ CUP (120 ML) KETCHUP

In a small bowl, add water to the tamarind concentrate and stir until a thin, smooth paste forms.

Heat the oil in a medium skillet over medium-high heat. Add the shallots and cook until soft. Remove the pan from the heat and add ¼ cup (60 ml) of the rum (do not pour straight from the bottle). If desired, use a long match to carefully light the rum (stand away from the pan, as flames may shoot upward), and shake the pan until the flame goes out. Scrape any loose bits from the bottom of the pan. Add the remaining ¼ cup (60 ml) rum and repeat the process. If you choose not to flambé, follow the same precaution, but add all the rum at once and cook for 2 to 3 minutes before adding the tamarind mixture, vinegar, and brown sugar. Simmer for 1 minute. Add the ketchup and simmer for about 15 minutes. Strain the glaze before using it.

RED BEANS AND COCONUT RICE

Makes 4 cups (1 L)

3 CUPS (720 ML) COOKED RICE

1 CUP (240 ML) COOKED RED BEANS, RINSED
    AND DRAINED

½ CUP (120 ML) COCONUT MILK

In a large saucepan over low heat, stir together the rice, beans, and coconut milk and cook for 8 to 10 minutes, until warmed through.

Conch Fritters with Banana-Guava Ketchup

CHEF CONNY ANDERSSON

Makes 8 servings

BANANA-GUAVA KETCHUP

1 TABLESPOON (15 ML) VEGETABLE OIL

½ WHITE ONION, CHOPPED

2 RIPE BANANAS, COARSELY CHOPPED

2 TABLESPOONS (30 ML) RAISINS

1 TABLESPOON (15 ML) MADRAS CURRY POWDER

½ CUP (120 ML) FRESH ORANGE JUICE

2 TABLESPOONS (30 ML) DISTILLED WHITE VINEGAR

2 TABLESPOONS (30 ML) FRESH LIME JUICE

¾ CUP (180 ML) GUAVA JUICE

2 TABLESPOONS (30 ML) DARK BROWN SUGAR

SALT AND FRESHLY GROUND BLACK PEPPER

FRITTERS

2 TABLESPOONS (30 ML) BUTTER

1 RIB CELERY, MINCED

½ WHITE ONION, MINCED

½ LARGE CARROT, MINCED

½ LEEK, MINCED

½ POUND (227 G) CONCH MEAT, CLEANED AND FINELY CHOPPED

PINCH OF DRIED THYME

PINCH OF DRIED BASIL

PINCH OF DRIED OREGANO

2 EGGS

½ TEASPOON (2.5 ML) BAKING POWDER

2 CUPS (480 ML) ALL-PURPOSE FLOUR

2 CLOVES GARLIC, MINCED

1 CUP (240 ML) MILK

SALT AND FRESHLY GROUND BLACK PEPPER

VEGETABLE OIL, FOR SAUTÉING

TO MAKE THE KETCHUP: Heat the oil in a skillet over medium-high heat. Add the onion and sauté for 5 to 7 minutes, until translucent. Reduce the heat to low, add the bananas, and cook for 5 minutes. Add the raisins, curry powder, orange juice, vinegar, lime juice, guava juice, and brown sugar and simmer for 15 minutes. Season with salt and pepper, then transfer to a food processor and blend until smooth.

TO MAKE THE FRITTERS: Melt the butter in a skillet over medium-high heat. Add the celery, onion, carrot, and leek and sauté just until soft. Remove from the heat. When the vegetables are cool, add the conch, thyme, basil, oregano, eggs, baking powder, flour, garlic, and milk. Season with the salt and pepper.

In a deep fryer, heat the oil to 350°F (180°C). Working in batches, gently slip the conch mixture into the oil by the tablespoonful and fry until golden brown, about 4 minutes. Transfer to paper towels to drain. Serve with the Banana-Guava Ketchup.

Ackee and Salt Fish with Johnnycakes

CHEF CONNY ANDERSSON

Makes 6 servings

½ POUND (227 G) SALTED CODFISH

3 TABLESPOONS (45 ML) VEGETABLE OIL

1 TEASPOON (5 ML) CHOPPED GARLIC

4 SCALLIONS, WHITE AND GREEN PARTS, CUT INTO THIN STRIPS

¼ WHITE ONION, DICED

½ RED BELL PEPPER, CUT INTO THIN STRIPS

½ GREEN BELL PEPPER, CUT INTO THIN STRIPS

½ TOMATO, PEELED, SEEDED, AND DICED

4 TABLESPOONS (60 ML) WATER

½ CAN (20 OUNCES [567 G]) ACKEE, STRAINED (SEE RESOURCES, PAGE 245)

2 TABLESPOONS (30 ML) BUTTER

1 SPRIG FRESH THYME, FINELY CHOPPED

1 HABANERO CHILE PEPPER, SEEDED AND DICED (SEE NOTE)

SALT AND FRESHLY GROUND BLACK PEPPER

JOHNNYCAKES (RECIPE FOLLOWS)

Place the fish into a large bowl with enough water to cover, and refrigerate overnight, changing the water three or four times.

Add the fish to a large pot of water, bring to a boil, and cook for 15 to 20 minutes, or until very soft and flaky. Drain thoroughly, then separate into coarse flakes, discarding the skin and bones. Set aside.

Heat the oil in a large skillet over medium-high heat. Add the garlic, scallions, onion, and bell peppers and cook until translucent, about 5 to 7 minutes. Add the fish, tomato, and 4 tablespoons (60 ml) water and bring to a boil. Gently fold in the ackee, then stir in the butter, thyme, and chile pepper and season to taste with the salt and pepper.

Serve with Johnnycakes.

NOTE: *Wear plastic gloves when handling chile peppers, and wash your hands thoroughly with soap and water before touching sensitive parts of your body, especially your face. To reduce the heat in the finished dish, use only the sides of the pepper (discard seeds and core).*

JOHNNYCAKES

Makes 36

3½ CUPS (840 ML) ALL-PURPOSE FLOUR

⅔ CUP (160 ML) GRATED COCONUT

1 TABLESPOON (15 ML) BAKING POWDER

1 TEASPOON (5 ML) SALT

6 TABLESPOONS (90 ML) BUTTER

⅓ CUP (80 ML) SUGAR

1 EGG

½ CUP (120 ML) MILK

VEGETABLE OIL

In a medium bowl, stir together the flour, coconut, baking powder, and salt. In another medium bowl, using an electric mixer, beat the butter and sugar until fluffy. Add the egg and beat until combined. Alternate adding half the flour mixture, then half the milk, stirring well after each addition. Gather the dough and roll out to a ¼" (0.6 cm) thickness on a lightly floured surface, then cut into rounds with a 2" (5 cm) cutter.

Heat at least 2" (5 cm) of oil in a large pot over medium-high heat to 360°F (182°C). Working in batches, gently slip the rounds into the oil and fry until golden brown. Transfer to paper towels to drain.

Serve warm or at room temperature.

Snapper Roasted in Banana Leaves with Mango–Black Bean Relish

CHEF CONNY ANDERSSON

Makes 4 servings

RELISH

1 RIPE MANGO, CUT INTO SMALL CUBES

¼ CUP (60 ML) CANNED BLACK BEANS, RINSED AND DRAINED

JUICE OF 2 LIMES

1 JALAPEÑO CHILE PEPPER, SEEDED AND CHOPPED (SEE NOTE)

1 TABLESPOON (15 ML) CHOPPED FRESH CILANTRO

¼ RED BELL PEPPER, CORED, SEEDED, AND FINELY DICED

2 SCALLIONS, WHITE AND GREEN PARTS, FINELY SLICED

1 TABLESPOON (15 ML) SIMPLE SYRUP (SEE NOTE)

SALT

SNAPPER

4 (12" [30 CM]-SQUARE) BANANA LEAVES (SEE RESOURCES, PAGE 245)

4 RED SNAPPER FILLETS, 3 OUNCES (85 G) EACH

JUICE OF 2 LIMES

2 TABLESPOONS (30 ML) CHOPPED FRESH CILANTRO

1 ROMA TOMATO, THINLY SLICED

HOT RED PEPPER SAUCE

SALT AND FRESHLY GROUND BLACK PEPPER

TO MAKE THE RELISH: In a large bowl, combine the mango, black beans, lime juice, chile pepper, cilantro, bell pepper, scallions, and syrup. Toss to combine, and season to taste with the salt. Let stand for at least 1 hour before serving

TO MAKE THE SNAPPER: Preheat the oven to 400°F (200°C).

Heat the banana leaves in a dry skillet or over an open flame until they become pliable. Place a fish fillet in the center of each and drizzle with the lime juice. Add a sprinkling of cilantro and 1 or 2 slices of tomato, then top with more cilantro and a dash of red pepper sauce. Season to taste with the salt and pepper and fold the leaves over the fish, securing both ends with wooden toothpicks.

Arrange the packets in a large baking dish and roast in the oven for 20 to 25 minutes, until the fish flakes easily. Before serving, split the banana leaves open and top with the relish.

NOTE: *Wear plastic gloves when handling chile peppers, and wash your hands thoroughly with soap and water before touching sensitive parts of your body, especially your face. To reduce the heat in the finished dish, use only the sides of the pepper (discard seeds and core).*

To make syrup, heat equal parts water and sugar over high heat until dissolved, or substitute honey for the syrup.

Conch Chowder

CHEF CONNY ANDERSSON

Makes 4 servings

3 TABLESPOONS (45 ML) BUTTER

½ POUND (227 G) CONCH MEAT, CLEANED AND COARSELY CHOPPED

½ LARGE CARROT, FINELY DICED

1 RIB CELERY, FINELY DICED

½ WHITE ONION, FINELY DICED

1 TEASPOON (5 ML) MINCED GARLIC

1 HABANERO CHILE PEPPER, SEEDED AND FINELY DICED (SEE NOTE)

3 TABLESPOONS (45 ML) ALL-PURPOSE FLOUR

4 CUPS (1 L) FISH STOCK

1 CUP (240 ML) HEAVY CREAM

1 TEASPOON (5 ML) GROUND ALLSPICE

½ TEASPOON (2.5 ML) GROUND NUTMEG

2 BAY LEAVES

½ TABLESPOON (7.5 ML) DRIED THYME

SALT AND FRESHLY GROUND BLACK PEPPER

Melt the butter in a large skillet over medium-high heat. Add the conch, carrot, celery, onion, garlic, and chile pepper and sauté for 5 to 7 minutes, until soft and translucent, but don't let the vegetables brown. Sprinkle with the flour and stir just until absorbed.

Add the stock and simmer for about 10 minutes. Add the cream, allspice, nutmeg, bay leaves, and thyme. Season to taste with the salt and pepper and cook a few minutes longer to let the flavors blend. Remove the bay leaves before serving.

NOTE: *Wear plastic gloves when handling chile peppers, and wash your hands thoroughly with soap and water before touching sensitive parts of your body, especially your face. To reduce the heat in the finished dish, use only the sides of the pepper (discard seeds and core).*

Tuna Tartare with Avocado and Pawpaw Salad

CHEF CONNY ANDERSSON

Makes 4 servings

JUICE OF 1 LIME

2 TABLESPOONS (30 ML) SOY SAUCE

1 TEASPOON (5 ML) SESAME OIL

2 SCALLIONS, WHITE AND GREEN PARTS, CHOPPED

½ TEASPOON (2.5 ML) GRATED FRESH GINGER

1 TABLESPOON (15 ML) CHOPPED FRESH CILANTRO

½ POUND (227 G) AHI TUNA, FINELY CHOPPED

1 AVOCADO, PEELED, PITTED, AND DICED

SALT AND FRESHLY GROUND BLACK PEPPER

PAWPAW SALAD (RECIPE FOLLOWS)

In a small bowl, combine the lime juice, soy sauce, oil, scallions, ginger, and cilantro. Just before serving, toss with the tuna and avocado. Season to taste with the salt and pepper and serve at once with Pawpaw Salad. (If tartare sits for more than 15 minutes, it will discolor and become mushy.)

PAWPAW SALAD

Makes 4 cups (1 L)

1 POUND (454 G) GREEN PAPAYA, PEELED AND THINLY SLICED INTO MATCHSTICK PIECES

JUICE OF 3 LIMES

3 TABLESPOONS (45 ML) CHOPPED FRESH CILANTRO

½ TEASPOON (2.5 ML) SEEDED AND MINCED HABANERO CHILE PEPPER (SEE NOTE)

2 TABLESPOONS (30 ML) SIMPLE SYRUP (SEE NOTE, PAGE 118)

1 TOMATO, PEELED, SEEDED, AND CHOPPED

SALT AND FRESHLY GROUND BLACK PEPPER

In a large bowl, combine the papaya, lime juice, cilantro, chile pepper, syrup, tomato, and salt and pepper to taste. Toss gently.

NOTE: *Wear plastic gloves when handling chile peppers, and wash your hands thoroughly with soap and water before touching sensitive parts of your body, especially your face. To reduce the heat in the finished dish, use only the sides of the pepper (discard seeds and core).*

Butter-Poached Spiny Lobster with Spinach and Mango Butter

CHEF CONNY ANDERSSON

Makes 2 servings

MANGO BUTTER

½ CUP (120 ML) DRY WHITE WINE

2 SHALLOTS

1 TABLESPOON (15 ML) DISTILLED WHITE VINEGAR

½ CUP (120 ML) FISH STOCK

1 BAY LEAF

1 SPRIG FRESH THYME

¼ CUP (60 ML) HEAVY CREAM

½ CUP (120 ML) MANGO PUREE

½ CUP (120 ML) BUTTER, AT ROOM TEMPERATURE

JUICE OF 1 LIME

SALT AND FRESHLY GROUND BLACK PEPPER

LOBSTER

2 SPINY LOBSTERS, 2½ POUNDS (1 KG) EACH, SPLIT

4 TABLESPOONS (60 ML) BUTTER

3 SHALLOTS, FINELY CHOPPED

4 SPRIGS FRESH THYME, CHOPPED

SALT AND FRESHLY GROUND BLACK PEPPER

1 POUND (454 G) FRESH SPINACH

TO MAKE THE MANGO BUTTER: In a medium saucepan over medium-high heat, combine the wine, shallots, vinegar, stock, bay leaf, and thyme. Bring to a boil and cook until reduced by half. Add the cream and puree and return to a boil. Add the butter 1 tablespoon (15 ml) at a time, stirring constantly. Stir in the lime juice and season with the salt and pepper. Strain and keep warm until ready to serve.

TO MAKE THE LOBSTER: Using a large chef's knife, split the lobsters in half lengthwise. Clean out the cavities and rinse well, then pull the meat out of the shells and cut into 1" (2.5 cm) chunks. In a pot of water, boil the shells until they turn orange. Set aside.

Melt the butter in a large skillet over medium heat. When it begins to foam, add the lobster, shallots, and thyme. Season to taste with the salt and pepper. Cook for 3 to 4 minutes, or until the lobster is opaque. Transfer to a plate.

Add the spinach to the pan and season with the salt and pepper. Cook for 1 to 2 minutes, or until wilted.

TO ASSEMBLE THE DISH: Fill the head portions of the shells with the spinach, and the tails with the lobster. Spoon the mango butter over the lobster.

Banana Beignets with Pineapple Carpaccio and Vanilla Bean Ice Cream

CHEF CONNY ANDERSSON

Makes 8 servings

ICE CREAM

2 FRESH VANILLA BEAN PODS

2 CUPS (480 ML) MILK

2 CUPS (480 ML) HEAVY CREAM

12 EGG YOLKS

1 CUP (240 ML) SUGAR

CARPACCIO

1 FRESH PINEAPPLE

¼ CUP (60 ML) SIMPLE SYRUP (SEE NOTE, PAGE 118)

½ CUP (120 ML) LIGHT BROWN SUGAR

BEIGNETS

1 CUP (240 ML) ALL-PURPOSE FLOUR

½ TEASPOON (2.5 ML) SALT

1 TEASPOON (5 ML) SUGAR

1 TEASPOON (5 ML) BAKING POWDER

2 LARGE EGGS

1 CUP (240 ML) WATER

¼ CUP (60 ML) SUGAR

2 TEASPOONS (10 ML) GROUND CINNAMON

VEGETABLE OIL

4 BANANAS, PEELED AND SLICED LENGTHWISE, THEN QUARTERED

TO MAKE THE ICE CREAM: Split the vanilla bean pods lengthwise and scrape out all the seeds. In a large saucepan, combine the milk and cream, add the seeds and pods, and bring to a slow boil over medium heat.

In a large bowl, using an electric mixer on high speed, beat the egg yolks and sugar for 2 to 3 minutes, until light and fluffy. Pour in half the boiling milk mixture and mix to combine. Pour into the pan and cook, stirring, over medium heat, until thick enough to coat the back of a spoon.

Remove from the heat and immediately strain into another large bowl. Place over a second large bowl filled with ice and let cool completely, stirring every 30 minutes. When cool, freeze in an ice cream maker according to the manufacturer's directions.

TO MAKE THE CARPACCIO: Cut off the top and tail of the pineapple and, following the shape of the fruit, slice off the skin with a serrated knife, making sure to remove all the eyes. Using a serrated knife, slice the fruit into the thinnest possible rings.

Place each slice onto a sheet of plastic wrap, brush with the syrup, rub the brown sugar over the surface, and top with a second sheet of plastic wrap. Repeat with the remaining slices, transfer to a rimmed baking sheet, and refrigerate overnight.

TO MAKE THE BEIGNETS: In a medium bowl, combine the flour, salt, sugar, and baking powder. Add the eggs and 1 cup (240 ml) water, and whisk until a smooth paste forms. Refrigerate for at least 1 hour.

In a small bowl, combine the sugar and cinnamon, and set aside.

In a deep fryer, heat the oil to 350°F (180°C). Working in batches, dip the bananas into the chilled batter and coat completely. Slip them into the oil and fry for about 2 minutes, or until golden brown. Transfer to paper towels to drain. Dust with cinnamon-sugar mixture.

TO ASSEMBLE THE DISH: Arrange equal portions of the carpaccio in an overlapping circle on a dessert plate. Lay two pieces of fried banana in the center, and top with one large scoop of vanilla ice cream. Drizzle with vanilla bean syrup.

THE FOUR SEASONS HOTEL

Beverly Hills, California

Ashley James, Executive Chef

"My parents visited the Grenadines on vacation, but that's as close as I've ever gotten!" admits Chef Ashley James, the only chef profiled in this book who has never worked in the Caribbean.

According to Chef James, all great chefs have been mentored, tutored, or influenced by a great chef who worked in the Caribbean—where freshness and mellow, sultry flavor is key.

James's culinary story began at the age of 15, when he went to work at a family friend's hotel in England. Then came culinary school, followed by classical training in France and a position at Jules Vernes, the Michelin star–awarded restaurant ensconced in the Eiffel Tower.

Time spent in Bordeaux gave him a true appreciation of the history and connectivity of wine and food. "There are usually subtle shades of change over the years in the history of a region's food. New flavors are introduced by visitors, marauders. It's fascinating," he says. This newfound fascination led to stints in Majorca, then India, and finally back to England, where he started a small company. "I thought I'd grow old there, selling wine—get fat and have a family."

But then came a call from Singapore and the Regent Hotel there (a Four Seasons property), and off James went to Maxim's of Singapore. He has been with the Four Seasons ever since, at Punta Mita, Mexico; then Buenos Aires; and now Beverly Hills.

To Chef James, cooking is intuitive, and balance is paramount. Through his travels, he has learned a great deal about what he calls lines of flavors, and he has great respect for the regional cuisines of the world. "I don't like to do too much mixing—everything should be going toward a sense of balance." So he bows to, but is also innovative with, local rules. "California is Asian with Latin influences—that is the culture. The changes you make should be subtle so that they are lasting and have influence. In the United States, we can get absolutely everything, but I like to source what we have locally and have the food reflect where you are in the world—using fresh California produce. And this is something that is the essence of Caribbean cooking, also—vanilla and coffee and fragrant fruits are key in Caribbean cooking because those foods are there.

"I respect the Caribbean gastronomical history. It's beautiful and it's ancient. I know this in my heart even if I haven't seen it firsthand."

Grenadian Tropical Fruit and Shrimp Ceviche with Crispy Sweet Potato Chips

FOUR SEASONS HOTEL, BEVERLY HILLS
EXECUTIVE CHEF ASHLEY JAMES

Makes 4 servings

SAUCE

2 TABLESPOONS (30 ML) OLIVE OIL

½ ONION, CHOPPED

2 CLOVES GARLIC, CHOPPED

2 TABLESPOONS (30 ML) CHOPPED FRESH GINGER

2 RIPE MANGOS, PEELED AND CUT INTO LARGE CUBES

½ CUP (120 ML) BROWN SUGAR

1 TABLESPOON (15 ML) MINCED GREEN CHILE PEPPER (SEE NOTE)

½ TEASPOON (2.5 ML) GROUND CUMIN

2 TABLESPOONS (30 ML) RED WINE VINEGAR

SALT AND FRESHLY GROUND BLACK PEPPER

2 CUPS (480 ML) MANGO NECTAR

CEVICHE

1 POUND (454 G) SHRIMP, PEELED AND DEVEINED, TAILS REMOVED

JUICE OF 6 LIMES

½ CUP (120 ML) PEELED, CORED, AND CHOPPED PINEAPPLE

½ CUP (120 ML) PEELED AND CHOPPED MANGO

½ CUP (120 ML) PEELED, SEEDED, AND CHOPPED PAPAYA

½ CUP (120 ML) CHOPPED TOMATOES

½ CUP (120 ML) CHOPPED ONION

½ CUP (120 ML) CHOPPED FRESH CILANTRO

CHIPS

VEGETABLE OIL

2 LARGE SWEET POTATOES

SALT

(CONTINUED)

TROPICAL FRUIT AND SHRIMP CEVICHE-CONTINUED

TO MAKE THE SAUCE: Heat the oil in a large saucepan over medium heat. Add the onion, garlic, and ginger and cook for 4 to 5 minutes, or until soft (do not brown). Stir in the mango, brown sugar, chile pepper, and cumin.

When the mixture starts to boil and looks like jam, reduce the heat and stir in the vinegar and salt and black pepper to taste. Cook for 5 minutes to let the flavors blend. Add the mango nectar and cook for 10 minutes. Transfer to a blender and process until smooth. Strain and refrigerate for up to 4 hours.

TO MAKE THE CEVICHE: In a large bowl, combine the shrimp and lime juice. Refrigerate for 30 minutes, then add the pineapple, mango, papaya, tomatoes, onion, and cilantro and toss to combine. Stir in the fruit sauce and serve chilled.

TO MAKE THE SWEET POTATOES: In a deep fryer, heat the oil to 360°F (182°C). Using a mandolin or very sharp knife, slice the sweet potatoes as thinly as possible. Slip the slices into the oil and fry on both sides until crisp. Transfer to paper towels to drain. Sprinkle with salt to taste.

TO ASSEMBLE THE DISH: Arrange the ceviche in a martini glass or on a serving plate. Garnish with sweet potato chips.

NOTE: *Wear plastic gloves when handling chile peppers, and wash your hands thoroughly with soap and water before touching sensitive parts of your body, especially your face. To reduce the heat in the finished dish, use only the sides of the pepper (discard seeds and core).*

Black Bean Soup with Tostones

FOUR SEASONS HOTEL, BEVERLY HILLS, EXECUTIVE CHEF ASHLEY JAMES

Makes 8 servings

SOUP

6 CUPS (1.4 L) WATER

1 POUND (454 G) DRIED BLACK BEANS

1 TABLESPOON (15 ML) CORN OIL

½ ONION, CHOPPED

6 SLICES BACON, CHOPPED

2 RIBS CELERY, CHOPPED

1 CARROT, CHOPPED

2 CLOVES GARLIC, CHOPPED

½ CUP (120 ML) CHOPPED CILANTRO

1 GREEN CHILE PEPPER, CHOPPED (SEE NOTE)

2 TEASPOONS (30 ML) GROUND CUMIN

SALT AND FRESHLY GROUND BLACK PEPPER

10 CUPS (2.3 L) CHICKEN STOCK

TOSTONES

VEGETABLE OIL

2 UNRIPE PLANTAINS, PEELED AND CUT INTO
    1" (2.5 CM)-THICK PIECES

SALT

GROUND CUMIN

GARNISH

CHOPPED CILANTRO

2 TABLESPOONS (30 ML) SOUR CREAM

TO MAKE THE SOUP: In a large pot, bring 6 cups (1.4 L) of water to a boil. Add the dried beans, lower the heat, and simmer for 2 to 3 minutes. Remove from heat, cover, and allow to stand for 4 to 6 hours.

Heat the oil in a saucepan over medium-high heat. Add the onion and bacon and cook for 5 minutes. Add the celery, carrot, and garlic and cook for another 5 minutes. Add the cilantro, chile pepper, and cumin and cook, stirring, until the cumin is absorbed. Season to taste with the salt and black pepper. Add the beans and stock and bring to a boil. Simmer for 45 minutes, or until the beans are soft, skimming off any foam that rises to the surface. Transfer to a blender and process until smooth.

TO MAKE THE TOSTONES: Heat at least 2" (5 cm) of oil in a large pot over medium-high heat to 360°F (182°C). Working in batches, gently slip the plantains into the oil and fry until golden brown. Transfer to a rack and let cool to room temperature. Flatten with a spatula or the flat side of a chef's knife, then return to the oil and fry in batches until crisp. Transfer to paper towels to drain, and sprinkle with the salt and cumin to taste. Add the tostones to the serving bowl of soup, then garnish it with the cilantro and sour cream.

NOTE: *Wear plastic gloves when handling chile peppers, and wash your hands thoroughly with soap and water before touching sensitive parts of your body, especially your face. To reduce the heat in the finished dish, use only the sides of the pepper (discard seeds and core).*

Grenadian Spice Cake
with Rum-Marinated Pineapple

EXECUTIVE CHEF ASHLEY JAMES

Makes 10 servings

CAKE

1⅓ CUPS (320 ML) RAW CANE SUGAR

¼ CUP (60 ML) MOLASSES

1½ TEASPOONS (7.5 ML) GRATED LIME ZEST

1 CUP (240 ML) UNSALTED BUTTER

3 EGGS

2¼ CUPS (540 ML) SIFTED ALL-PURPOSE FLOUR

¾ TEASPOON (3.7 ML) BAKING POWDER

1 TEASPOON (5 ML) GROUND NUTMEG

½ TEASPOON (2.5 ML) GROUND CINNAMON

¼ TEASPOON (1.2 ML) GROUND ALLSPICE

½ CUP (120 ML) MILK

⅛ TEASPOON (0.6 ML) SALT

PINEAPPLE

1 PINEAPPLE, PEELED AND CORED

2 FRESH VANILLA BEAN PODS

1 CUP (240 ML) SUGAR

2 CUPS (480 ML) WATER

½ CUP (120 ML) GRENADIAN RUM

⅔ CUP (160 ML) PINEAPPLE JAM

WHIPPED CREAM (OPTIONAL)

COCONUT SORBET (OPTIONAL)

TO MAKE THE CAKE: Preheat the oven to 350°F (180°C). Coat an 8" (20 cm) round cake pan with butter or cooking spray.

In a medium bowl, using an electric mixer, cream together the sugar, molasses, lime zest, and butter until light and fluffy. Beat in the eggs one at a time. Gently fold in the flour, baking powder, nutmeg, cinnamon, allspice, milk, and salt to form a smooth, fluffy batter.

Pour into the prepared pan and bake for 25 to 35 minutes, or until a toothpick inserted into the center comes out clean. Cool in the pan for 10 minutes, then turn out onto a rack to cool completely.

TO MAKE THE PINEAPPLE: Cut the pineapple lengthwise into 4 pieces, then slice into ¼" (0.6 cm) pieces.

Split the vanilla pods lengthwise and scrape out the seeds with a small spoon, then place the seeds and pods into a small saucepan over medium-high heat. Add the sugar and 2 cups (480 ml) water and bring to a gentle boil. Add the pineapple, reduce the heat to low, and simmer for 3 minutes, or until the liquid is syrupy.

Remove the pan from the heat and add the rum. Transfer to a bowl and refrigerate before serving. (You can make the pineapple 1 or 2 days in advance.)

TO ASSEMBLE THE DESSERT: Cut the cake into 3 layers. Place the bottom layer in a 9" (23 cm) cake or spring-form pan, spoon on ¼ cup (60 ml) pineapple syrup, then spread lightly with the jam. Repeat with the other layers, then pour ¼ cup (60 ml) syrup on the top of the cake. Cover with plastic wrap and refrigerate for at least 2 hours, or up to overnight.

Slice the cake and serve with the pineapple and whipped cream or coconut sorbet.

ELIZABETH'S,
THE PALMS AT PELICAN COVE

Christiansted, St. Croix

Jason Gould, Chef

The best local food is often found off the beaten path in small, family-owned restaurants. A shining example of new restaurant owners who carry on this tradition are Jason and Elizabeth Gould, who own and operate Elizabeth's at the Palms.

Fresh fish is, quite naturally, a central theme at Elizabeth's. "Mahi mahi and wahoo are very popular at most of the restaurants on the island," says Gould. One of Gould's favorite dishes is Coconut-Saffron Mussels. "It's true that the mussels come in from off-island," he explains, "but the sauce is made with Cruzan rum. We're loyal to the native products, and they're loyal to us." Cruzan rums—produced since the 18th century on St. Croix—are aged for 2 years, and some for 12 years or more, and are widely praised as smooth, unique, and full flavored. "Caribbean Blackjack Pasta is another big hit in our restaurant," continues Gould. "The seafood really stands up to the sauce."

Although Jason and Elizabeth weren't around for Hurricane Hugo, which struck St. Croix in 1989, they are very much aware of the destruction it caused. "The locals still talk about Hugo. As I travel over the island to get supplies for the restaurant, I can still see devastation from it—places that haven't been brought back to life. Since Elizabeth and I have been here, we haven't had more than severe rains, some harsh winds—we lose power occasionally if the heavy rains come. But we all live in paradise, and you have to take the good with the bad."

Coconut-Saffron Mussels

ELIZABETH'S, CHEF JASON GOULD

Makes 1 serving

1 TEASPOON (5 ML) BUTTER

2–3 CLOVES GARLIC, CHOPPED

3 TABLESPOONS (45 ML) CHOPPED SHALLOT

1 DOZEN NEW ZEALAND MUSSELS, SCRUBBED

3 TABLESPOONS (45 ML) CRUZAN COCONUT RUM

½ CUP (120 ML) HEAVY CREAM

3 STRANDS SAFFRON

2 TABLESPOONS (30 ML) COCO LOPEZ

SALT AND FRESHLY GROUND BLACK PEPPER

COCONUT SHELL (OPTIONAL)

Melt the butter in a large skillet over medium-high heat. Add the garlic and shallot and cook for 2 to 3 minutes, or until lightly browned. Add the mussels and toss to coat. Remove the pan from the heat and add the rum (do not pour straight from the bottle). If desired, use a long match to carefully light the rum (stand away from the pan, as flames may shoot upward), and shake the pan until the flame goes out. If you choose not to flambé, follow the same directions for adding the rum and cook for 2 to 3 minutes, until the mussels open. Add the cream, saffron, and Coco Lopez and cook until the sauce begins to thicken, for 2 to 3 minutes longer. Season to taste with the salt and pepper. If serving in a coconut shell, line it with the mussels, discarding any that didn't open, and top with the sauce. Otherwise, spoon the mussels and sauce onto a plate.

Caribbean Blackjack Pasta

ELIZABETH'S, CHEF JASON GOULD

Makes 4 servings

2 TABLESPOONS (30 ML) BUTTER

2 TABLESPOONS (30 ML) CHOPPED GARLIC

2 TABLESPOONS (30 ML) CHOPPED SHALLOT

1 SMALL RED ONION, FINELY CHOPPED

½ POUND (227 G) OKRA, SLICED INTO RINGS

⅓ CUP (80 ML) DRY SHERRY

18 MUSSELS, SCRUBBED

½ DOZEN LARGE SEA SCALLOPS

½ DOZEN LARGE SHRIMP

¼ POUND (113 G) CRAWFISH

¾ CUP (180 ML) HEAVY CREAM

1 LARGE RED BELL PEPPER, CORED, SEEDED, AND DICED

SALT AND FRESHLY GROUND BLACK PEPPER

½ TEASPOON (2.5 ML) OLD BAY SEASONING

TABASCO SAUCE

16 OUNCES (454 G) RIGATONI, COOKED ACCORDING TO PACKAGE DIRECTIONS

Melt the butter in a large skillet over medium-high heat. Add the garlic and shallot and cook until golden brown. Add the onion and okra, then reduce the heat to medium and cook for 5 minutes, or until soft. If the vegetables stick to the pan, deglaze it with a small amount of the sherry.

Add the mussels, scallops, shrimp, and crawfish and toss to coat. Remove the pan from the heat and add the sherry (do not pour straight from the bottle). If desired, use a long match to carefully light the sherry (stand away from the pan, as flames may shoot upward), and shake the pan until the flame goes out. If you choose not to flambé, follow the same directions for adding the sherry and cook for 2 to 3 minutes, until the shrimp are pink and the mussels open.

Add the cream and bell pepper. Cook until the sauce begins to thicken. Remove the seafood to a plate or bowl, increase the heat, and cook until the sauce is reduced by half. Season with the salt, black pepper, Old Bay Seasoning, and Tabasco. Toss the seafood and sauce with the rigatoni and serve immediately.

ANGUILLA

Kevin Bacon

WELCOME HOME

Although he made his film debut in *Animal House,* now a cult comedy classic, Kevin Bacon first earned critical attention for his role in *Diner,* directed by Barry Levinson. Later, with *Footloose*, he became a mainstream star. Since then, just a few of his most notable and charismatic roles have been in *JFK,* directed by Oliver Stone; *A Few Good Men; Apollo 13; In the Cut; Mystic River; Where the Truth Lies;* and *The River Wild,* for which he earned a Golden Globe nomination.

A man of many talents, Kevin teamed up with his older brother, Michael, in 1995 to form the Bacon Brothers, a band that has released several successful albums. In 1996, seeking yet another new challenge, he made his directorial debut with the Showtime original movie *Losing Chase,* starring his wife, Kyra Sedgwick; Beau Bridges; and Helen Mirren. The film was screened at the Sundance Film Festival and won a Golden Globe and was nominated for two others, including one for Best Motion Picture Made for Television.

When taking a break from his busy career, Kevin makes regular trips to Anguilla, one of the most pristine islands of the Caribbean, with Kyra and their two teenage children, Travis and Sosie Ruth. The Bacons discovered Anguilla when their children were just babies and have vacationed there frequently ever since. They look forward to hearing the people of the island say "Welcome home!" each time they return.

Kevin and his family first visited the island more than a decade ago when they took the ferry over from St. Maarten for the day and were greeted by herds of roaming goats. Not as lush and tropical as much of the rest of the Caribbean, Anguilla's lack of vegetation has earned it the nickname "the rock," but the beaches are beautiful and pristine, and the warm water is home to an abundance of colorful tropical fish. "The island has had an unusual history," Kevin says. "It was originally colonized by the British and functioned as a plantation economy. But because the land was so barren, the British freed the slaves way back in the 19th century. As a result, the Anguillans have owned the land for generations."

In addition to the warmth of its people, Kevin and his family were attracted to Anguilla's laid-back lifestyle and the privacy it affords because its harbor can't accommodate the giant cruise ships that dock at other Caribbean vacation spots.

For the Bacon family, "doing very little" is a true luxury. They swim, scuba dive, explore some of the more remote beaches, visit with friends they have made on previous trips, and stock up on grocery items from the local markets. But a lot of their experience centers around "unbelievably great restaurants," and there are three that Kevin particularly loves.

"The Dune Preserve is kind of a shack that was built by a friend of mine named Bankie Banx, who I call the Anguillan Bob Dylan," explains Kevin. "He's a singer/songwriter who was raised on the island and has recorded several albums. Bankie is a phenomenal musician who has a club that's put together from old pieces of boat and driftwood and things that kind of wash up on the beach. At lunchtime, he grills fresh fish, ribs, or chicken with rice and peas. Eating and hanging out there, visiting with friends, listening to music, and learning about the history of the island from Bankie is an absolutely perfect afternoon.

"One of my favorite island fish is fresh red snapper that the local fishermen have caught that day," Kevin says. "I love it served whole, with the head on, accompanied by peas and rice."

Another favorite dining spot is Scilly Cay, which is located on a small island and accessible only by boat or helicopter. "The boatman picks you up and takes you to this unbelievable little paradise they've created that reminds me of Gilligan's Island. Scilly Cay serves lobster, chicken, or crawfish

prepared in a slightly spicy curry sauce. It is absolutely the best sauce I have ever tasted, and the three dishes are served with fresh fruit and pasta salad. Both the lobster and crawfish are Caribbean, or spiny, which means there isn't any claw meat, so you only eat the tail, which is succulent and flavorful even though the spines can rip your fingers apart."

Once you've eaten—or before—you can snorkel in the blue, blue water. "We've spotted giant turtles when snorkeling right offshore," says Kevin.

Rounding out the trio of eateries is the Fat Cat Gourmet, a local establishment with delicious baked goods that also serves baked chicken and "amazing coleslaw with a very tasty dressing!"

In the evenings, Kevin loves to hang out with other musically inclined natives and visitors at the beautiful little harbor at Sandy Ground, listening to the various bands. "It's almost as if they are in sync with each other, and when one band ends, another starts at a different location," he says.

To Kevin, Anguilla, with its remarkable food, good friends, good music, and pristine beaches, is a bit of paradise found and a wonderful place to "come home" to.

FATHER'S OFFICE

Los Angeles, California

Sang Yoon, Proprietor/Chef

Chef Sang Yoon's fabulous fare has graced the tables of some of the most noteworthy restaurants throughout the United States and in Europe. As executive chef for various Wolfgang Puck restaurants as well as Michael's in Los Angeles and New York, and with a stint as the chef behind glittering Hollywood events—including the post–Academy Awards Governor's Ball—Sang has tempted the taste buds of "royalty," including Dustin Hoffman, Steven Spielberg, Tom Hanks, Barbra Streisand, and Sting.

With years of experience in Caribbean cooking, Sang knows the flavors and subtleties of the islands. As a consultant to Virgin Atlantic Airlines, he prepared many island dishes and created menus on Necker Island for the airline's kitchen and CEO Richard Branson. In addition, he has been a guest and featured chef at Epicurean Week, held each year on the beautiful island of Anguilla, which each night pairs a different chef with a different winemaker.

Caribbean Whole Red Snapper with Honey-Roasted Plantains and Spicy Papaya Relish

CHEF SANG YOON, FATHER'S OFFICE

Makes 4 servings

1 RED SNAPPER (ABOUT 4 POUNDS [1.8 KG]), CLEANED AND SCALES REMOVED

6 TABLESPOONS (90 ML) GARLIC AND HERB–INFUSED OLIVE OIL (RECIPE FOLLOWS)

3 TABLESPOONS (45 ML) CARIBBEAN DRY SPICE RUB (RECIPE FOLLOWS)

SEA SALT

GROUND WHITE PEPPER

ROASTED PLANTAINS (RECIPE FOLLOWS)

SPICY PAPAYA RELISH (RECIPE FOLLOWS)

JUICE OF 6 FRESH KEY LIMES OR 2 REGULAR LIMES

GARLIC AND HERB–INFUSED OLIVE OIL

⅓ CUP (80 ML) EXTRA-VIRGIN OLIVE OIL

4 CLOVES GARLIC, CHOPPED

LEAVES FROM 1 (2" [5 CM]) SPRIG OF FRESH ROSEMARY, CHOPPED

1 TABLESPOON (15 ML) CHOPPED FRESH THYME LEAVES

CARIBBEAN DRY SPICE RUB

2 TABLESPOONS (30 ML) GROUND ALLSPICE

1 TABLESPOON (15 ML) GROUND CUMIN

1 TABLESPOON (15 ML) SMOKED SPANISH PAPRIKA

1 TABLESPOON (15 ML) GROUND ANCHO CHILE PEPPER

½ TABLESPOON (7.5 ML) MADRAS CURRY POWDER

ROASTED PLANTAINS

2 LARGE PLANTAINS, PEELED AND CUT CROSSWISE INTO 1" (2.5 CM) PIECES

2 TABLESPOONS (30 ML) HONEY THINNED WITH 2 TABLESPOONS (30 ML) ORANGE JUICE

1 TABLESPOON (15 ML) OLIVE OIL

FINE-GROUND SEA SALT

SPICY PAPAYA RELISH

3 CUPS (720 ML) PEELED AND DICED PAPAYA

¼ CUP (60 ML) CHOPPED FRESH CILANTRO

¼ CUP (60 ML) CHOPPED RED ONION

2 JALAPEÑO CHILE PEPPERS, SEEDED AND CHOPPED (SEE NOTE)

¼ CUP (60 ML) CHOPPED FLAT-LEAF PARSLEY

3 TABLESPOONS (45 ML) EXTRA-VIRGIN OLIVE OIL

JUICE OF 6 FRESH KEY LIMES OR 2 REGULAR LIMES

SEA SALT

GROUND WHITE PEPPER

(CONTINUED)

TO MAKE THE SNAPPER: Preheat a charcoal grill until the coals are very hot or a gas grill on high for 15 minutes.

Pat the fish dry inside and out with paper towels and make 6 deep, evenly spaced vertical cuts on each side, starting just behind the gills and working all the way to the tail. Lightly brush both sides of the fish with the oil, then rub both sides with the spice rub. Season to taste with the salt and pepper.

Place the fish on the grill rack and cover the grill. Cook for 10 minutes on each side, or until opaque, turning only once. (You can use a special fish-grilling basket to prevent sticking if your grill doesn't get very hot.) Remove from the heat and let stand for 3 minutes. Serve on a bed of Roasted Plantains and Spicy Papaya Relish, drizzled with the lime juice and the remaining oil.

TO MAKE THE OLIVE OIL: In a small saucepan, combine the oil, garlic, rosemary, and thyme and heat on the lowest possible stovetop setting for about 5 minutes, or until warm (do not boil). Remove from the heat and set aside to cool until ready to use.

TO MAKE THE RUB: In a small bowl, combine the allspice, cumin, paprika, chile pepper, and curry powder and mix well. Store leftover rub in a tightly covered jar for up to 2 months.

TO MAKE THE PLANTAINS: Preheat the oven to 450°F (230°C).

In a medium bowl, toss the plantains with the honey mixture and olive oil, and season lightly with the salt. Place in a shallow baking dish, cover with foil, and roast for 30 minutes or until very tender. Keep covered until ready to serve.

TO MAKE THE RELISH: In a large bowl, combine the papaya, cilantro, onion, chile peppers, parsley, oil, and lime juice and toss gently. Season to taste with the salt and white pepper, then cover and refrigerate until ready to serve. You can make the relish up to 6 hours in advance.

NOTE: *Wear plastic gloves when handling chile peppers, and wash your hands thoroughly with soap and water before touching sensitive parts of your body, especially your face. To reduce the heat in the finished dish, use only the sides of the pepper (discard seeds and core).*

Katie Couric

AN ISLAND GIRL AT HEART

Katie Couric is one of the best known and most respected television journalists in the country. Couric recently concluded a 15-year tenure as coanchor of NBC's *Today* show and assumes the role of anchor and managing editor of the *CBS Evening News* in the fall of 2006. An insightful interviewer who isn't afraid to take chances, she is as comfortable speaking with world leaders as she is talking with "real" people who have something important to say.

In May 2001, Katie was honored with a prestigious George Foster Peabody Award for her series "Confronting Colon Cancer." She has made colon cancer awareness a major focus of her work both on and off the air. In March 2000, with Lilly Tartikoff and the Entertainment Industry Foundation, she launched the National Colorectal Cancer Research Alliance (NCCRA), and she now spearheads an annual colon cancer awareness campaign during the month of March. Morgan Freeman appeared in a campaign public service announcement in 2005.

Katie remembers going on her first Caribbean cruise when she was in 9th grade and winning the ship's talent contest for the modern dance number she performed. More than 30 years later, some of her favorite family memories revolve around the times that she and her late husband, Jay Monohan, and their daughters, Ellie and Carrie, spent on the islands.

A decade after winning that talent contest on a family cruise to the Bahamas, Katie flew to St. Thomas and was enchanted by the island's bright colors and fascinating characters. "I remember finding a beautiful beach called Megan's Bay and really falling in love with the Caribbean there," she says. "Going into town at night, the colors were so vibrant, and the outdoor straw markets were full of life. My friends and I had a drink with novelist Robert Ludlum, and what a thrill that was! He was my first celebrity sighting and very charming."

More recently, Katie has been to the islands with her family during the girls' spring break, and one trip in particular stands out. "I recently came across an old video that was taken by a friend when we went to Barbados; it's full of footage of my husband, Jay, with our daughters, Ellie and Carrie. Jay was diagnosed with cancer about a month after we returned, and Carrie has watched that videotape at least a hundred times since I found it.

My friend gave it to me after Jay died, and I'd tucked it away until recently. We were never big on taking videos on vacation, so this one is precious.

"There are scenes from our trip to the zoo, eating out, playing on the beach; you can hear the sounds of the ocean and the birds. Popping that tape into the VCR brings back a flood of memories that are incredibly meaningful for me and for my girls."

After Jay's death, Katie and her daughters continued what had become a family tradition of visiting the Caribbean islands. On a trip to Jamaica, they stayed in Ian Fleming's home, which had just been converted into a resort fittingly called Goldeneye. "That was a fun trip. A friend of one of the friends we were traveling with was an executive with Island Records and knew the man reputed to make the best jerk chicken in all of Jamaica. We drove for about 45 minutes to get to his home, and it was fabulous!"

Katie and her children appreciate the wide-open spaces on the islands and the feeling of freedom that comes with them. "New York City apartment living is wonderful in many ways, but the opportunity to be outside and explore is a terrific change of pace. I love the sense of not knowing what I'm going to see and sharing the unexpected with my kids. The simplest things, like collecting shells, become special experiences.

"When you have nothing that you *have* to do, you can really enjoy just being together. Things like looking at the Caribbean nighttime sky, where you can see the stars and constellations so clearly, are such a treat. You can talk, dream, and not do much of anything except soak up the beauty around you."

Although Katie's dining experiences may not be her most cherished memories, she does greatly enjoy Caribbean cooking, especially the fresh fish and seafood. She also loves the fresh exotic fruits and island spices. "I love fresh fruit, guava juice especially, which you don't really drink in the States, and I love to knock a coconut from the tree, crack it open, and drink the milk inside." Something of a culinary adventurer, she appreciates Thai seasonings such as lemongrass, coconut milk, and ginger and the tanginess of hot, spicy dishes like jerk chicken.

One of Katie's favorite restaurants, Blanchard's, is on the island of Anguilla. Consistently considered one of the best eating establishments in the Caribbean by visitors and food critics alike, the cuisine is creative and sophisticated, with flavors from the islands, Asia, America, and the Mediterranean. Katie particularly remembers the jerk shrimp and one of her all-time favorite island indulgences, Blanchard's chocolate and coconut ice cream dessert. "The coconut ice cream dessert with the chocolate shell is a really cool thing because the chef lets the children help pour the chocolate over the balloons. Then, after it hardens, they pop and discard the balloons and fill the chocolate bowls with coconut ice cream and fresh coconut. It's like a frozen Mounds bar and really, really good."

The family also experienced some wonderful home cooking when they traveled to Nassau in the Bahamas. Emily Aranha, who helped take care of the girls as babies in New York, is Bahamian, and Katie, Carrie, and Ellie went to her home in Nassau, where they enjoyed traditional conch fritters. "Emily's whole extended family was there, and everyone was so gracious and hospitable. That was another really memorable visit.

"The only place I truly unwind is on the beach," Katie continues. "My perfect day would be getting up, having breakfast outside on my balcony, and watching the finches that are trying to steal my muffin while I'm planning our lunch or dinner. Next, I would take a snorkeling trip out into the ocean with my girls. Not knowing what you'll see makes it a different adventure every time. I find snorkeling so relaxing; I like being able to hear myself breathe."

Blanchard's Jerk Shrimp

BLANCHARD'S RESTAURANT, BOB AND MELINDA BLANCHARD

Jerk sauce is spicy-hot by definition, but you can vary the heat by increasing or reducing the amount of pepper. Blanchard's also serves the sauce spooned over chicken and pork and usually accompanies it with sweet potato puree to balance the spiciness.

Makes 8 servings (2¼ cups [540 ml] sauce)

SAUCE

1 TABLESPOON (15 ML) GROUND ALLSPICE

1 TEASPOON (5 ML) DRIED BASIL

1 TEASPOON (5 ML) GROUND CINNAMON

1 TEASPOON (5 ML) GROUND NUTMEG

1 TABLESPOON (15 ML) DRIED THYME

1 TEASPOON (5 ML) CAYENNE PEPPER, OR TO TASTE

1 TABLESPOON (15 ML) + 1 TEASPOON (5 ML) SALT

1 TEASPOON (5 ML) FRESHLY GROUND BLACK PEPPER

1 TABLESPOON (15 ML) LIGHT BROWN SUGAR

¼ CUP (60 ML) OLIVE OIL

¼ CUP (60 ML) SOY SAUCE

¾ CUP (180 ML) CIDER VINEGAR

½ CUP (120 ML) FRESH ORANGE JUICE

2 TABLESPOONS (60 ML) FRESH LIME JUICE

1 SCOTCH BONNET CHILE PEPPER, SEEDED AND MINCED (SEE NOTE)

1 SMALL ONION, MINCED

3 SCALLIONS, WHITE AND GREEN PARTS, THINLY SLICED

SHRIMP

2 POUNDS (1 KG) LARGE SHRIMP, PEELED AND DEVEINED, WITH TAILS

SALT AND FRESHLY GROUND BLACK PEPPER

CAYENNE PEPPER (OPTIONAL)

Preheat the grill or broiler.

TO MAKE THE SAUCE: In a medium saucepan over medium heat, combine the allspice, basil, cinnamon, nutmeg, thyme, cayenne, salt, pepper, and brown sugar and mix well. Slowly whisk in the oil, soy sauce, vinegar, orange juice, and lime juice. Add the chile pepper, onion, and scallions and stir to mix thoroughly. Cook until warmed through.

TO MAKE THE SHRIMP: Season the shrimp to taste with the salt, black pepper, and a little cayenne, if desired. Grill for 3 to 4 minutes, or until cooked through. Top with the sauce and serve immediately.

NOTE: *Wear plastic gloves when handling Scotch bonnet chiles, and wash your hands thoroughly with soap and water before touching sensitive parts of your body, especially your face. To reduce the heat in the finished dish, use only the sides of the pepper (discard the seeds and core).*

Blanchard's Cracked Coconut

BLANCHARD'S RESTAURANT, BOB AND MELINDA BLANCHARD

This is by far the most popular dessert at Blanchard's Restaurant. It's an elaborate recipe but so much fun to make that it's worth the time. You'll need to have some balloons on hand, but that just guarantees that the kids will want to help. To save time, you can substitute store-bought ice cream for homemade.

Makes 8 servings

8 SMALL WATER BALLOONS

12 OUNCES (340 G) SEMISWEET CHOCOLATE

4 OUNCES (113 G) BITTERSWEET CHOCOLATE

SHREDDED UNSWEETENED COCONUT

COCONUT ICE CREAM (RECIPE FOLLOWS), OR ANY KIND YOU PREFER

½ CUP (120 ML) KAHLUA CUSTARD SAUCE (RECIPE FOLLOWS)

Blow up the balloons, but not completely (the diameter at the widest part should be about 4" [11 cm]), and tie the tops. Line a baking sheet with parchment paper.

Melt the semisweet and bittersweet chocolate in the top of a double boiler over simmering water over low heat, stirring occasionally. Remove from the heat and let cool to room temperature. (If the chocolate is too hot when it touches the balloons, the balloons may pop, spattering chocolate all over the kitchen.)

Meanwhile, in a dry skillet over medium heat, toast the coconut, stirring often, for 3 to 4 minutes, or until golden.

Holding each balloon by the knot, dip it into the chocolate and roll gently until the chocolate covers half of each balloon. Arrange on a prepared baking sheet and place in the freezer for at least 10 minutes, or until the chocolate hardens. Remove from the freezer and repeat. Sprinkle the coconut onto the chocolate, covering as much as possible. Return to the refrigerator and allow to harden completely, for at least 30 minutes.

When the chocolate has hardened, pop the balloons with the point of a knife and quickly peel them from the chocolate. Refrigerate the chocolate bowls until ready to fill.

Let the ice cream soften at room temperature and spoon into 4 of the bowls, filling each a little more than halfway. Place the filled "coconuts" in the freezer until the ice cream is firm.

To serve, scoop out a hole about the size of a golf ball in the center of the ice cream. Position each filled "coconut" on a large plate and fill the hole with custard sauce. Lean an empty shell against the filled one so it looks as if the "coconut" has just been cracked open.

(CONTINUED)

BLANCHARD'S COCONUT ICE CREAM

This recipe is for true coconut lovers: There are bits of coconut in every bite. And unlike most homemade ice cream mixtures, this involves no cooking, which makes it a breeze to prepare. If you like, you can toast the coconut in a dry skillet before adding it to the mixture.

Makes about 1 quart (1 L)

1¼ CUPS (300 ML) CREAM OF COCONUT

1 CUP (240 ML) WHOLE MILK

¾ CUP (180 ML) HEAVY CREAM

¾ CUP (180 ML) SHREDDED UNSWEETENED COCONUT

In a large bowl, whisk together the cream of coconut, milk, cream, and coconut. Refrigerate until thoroughly chilled. Mix well and freeze in an ice cream maker according to the manufacturer's directions.

BLANCHARD'S KAHLUA CUSTARD SAUCE

Makes 2 cups (480 ml)

½ CUP (120 ML) WHOLE MILK

1 CUP (240 ML) HEAVY CREAM

¼ CUP (60 ML) SUGAR

3 LARGE EGG YOLKS, AT ROOM TEMPERATURE

PINCH OF SALT

1 TEASPOON (5 ML) VANILLA EXTRACT

3 TABLESPOONS (45 ML) KAHLUA

In a large saucepan over medium heat, bring the milk and cream to a boil. Remove from the heat and whisk in about half the sugar. In a large bowl, combine the remaining sugar, the egg yolks, and salt and set aside.

Return the cream mixture to medium heat. When it starts to simmer, reduce the heat, pour a ladleful of the cream mixture slowly into the egg yolks, whisking constantly, then return the yolk mixture to the cream and whisk for 3 minutes, or until thick enough to coat the back of a spoon. Add the vanilla extract and Kahlua and mix well. Pour through a fine sieve into a shallow bowl and refrigerate until cold. Serve immediately.

ST. BARTH'S

ST. BARTH'S

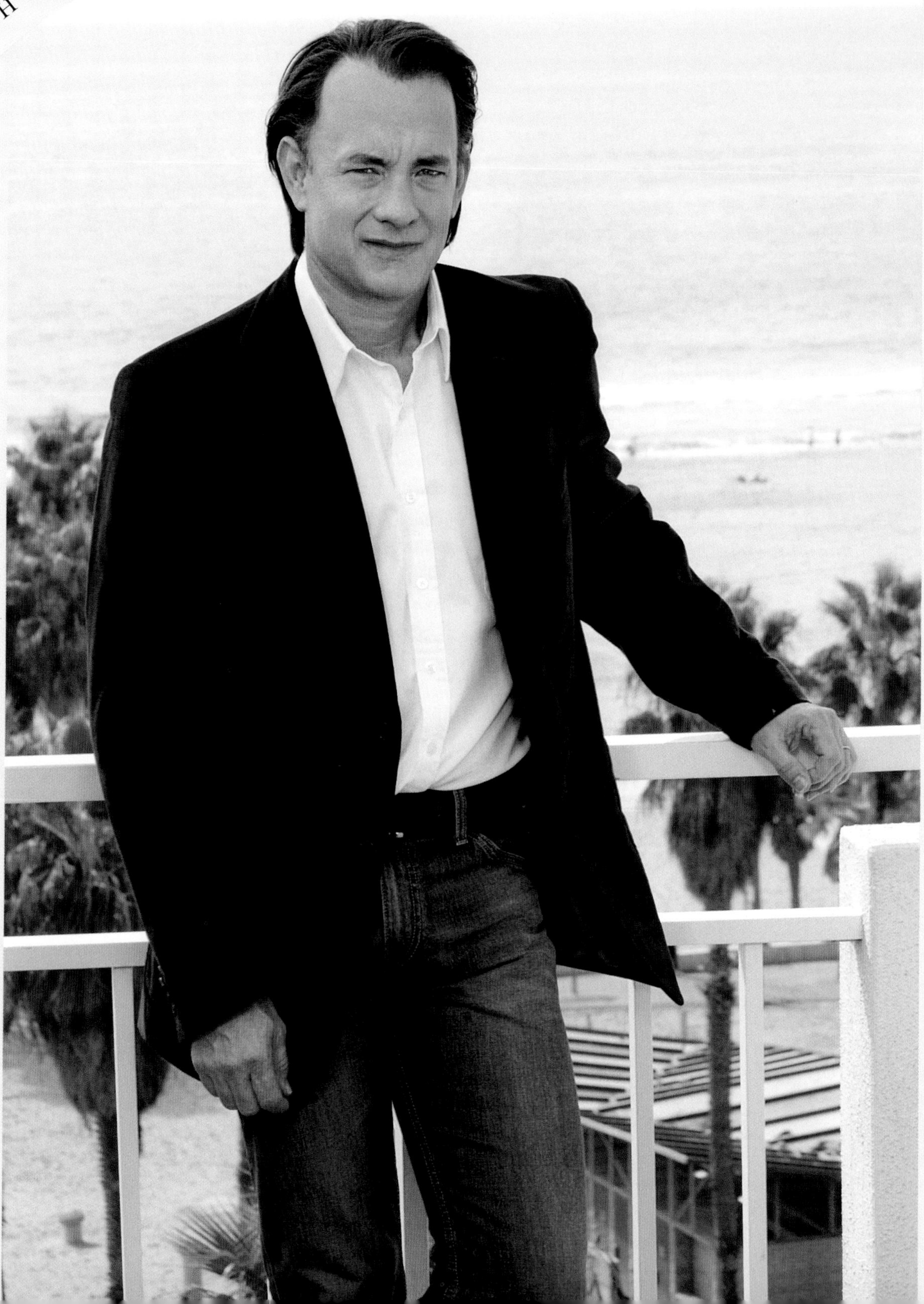

Tom Hanks

An Idyllic Hideaway

In addition to being a dedicated, award-winning actor, Tom Hanks is a humanitarian and a patriot of the highest order. Having spent the better part of his professional life raising money and awareness for AIDS, he then framed that work with a daring performance in the feature film *Philadelphia*. More recently, he capped off his stellar performance in *Saving Private Ryan* by helping to build a national monument to the men and women who served in World War II.

Tom's onscreen career is a reflection of his own ethical code—it's not easy to pull off. So when he and his family visit their favorite island, St. Barth's, it's to put work aside— "hide out," as he puts it—and relax. St. Barth's, with its many hidden coves and diverse beaches, is just the place to do that.

Tom and his wife, producer/actress Rita Wilson, and their family have spent quite a bit of time on the island, which—tiny as it is—offers many luxurious amenities to give them the experience of a resort retreat. Extravagant shops and boutiques, massages, and spa services are available and encouraged as relaxation takes on a unique, European flair here in the middle of the Caribbean. When Christopher Columbus first landed on the island, he named it Barthelemy, after his map-making brother, Bartholomeo. Later, the island was traded to Sweden, and at one point the island almost became an American colony, but in modern times, it's the French influence that dominates—in both its language and its magnificent food.

"Before our first visit, I thought of the islands as places where other people went to have adventures. You know—sailors and jetsetters; cruise patrons and crewmen," Tom admits. "But to enjoy the islands in person—with the family—I've got to say, it's just been a great joy. And lifetime memories are made every time we go there."

Tom is referring to St. Barth's, or St. Barthelemy, as it's formally known—an idyllic haven whose tiny population of about 7,000 is mostly descended from Swedish, English, and French settlers who followed Columbus to its shores. Hanks states that the Swedish and French were "the parts that stuck" and consequently have influenced the island's language and culture.

"I proposed to my wife on St. Barth's," Tom explains. "We also celebrated our first wedding anniversary in the very restaurant where it happened. So St. Barth's has been both the romantic getaway and the great family adventure for us.

"I've toted my kids up and down the paths to the beaches and had thin pizzas at midnight, mussels on Thursday nights, and seen the Bastille Day fireworks light up the harbor—with first two kids, then three.

"My wife, Rita, speaks French, which is always a good opener," he goes on, "especially with the 'regular folks'—people who have raised their kids there, those who come and go from Guadalupe, couples from France who are passionate about the wine shops—whom we've met over time just by being regulars in the stores and the town."

One of many things Tom and his wife enjoy is sampling the Creole-style cuisine featured in many of the island's restaurants. "The best native foods—like the Creole cuisine—come from that little café you discover by accident and keep going back to again and again for a particular spicy fish dish. And the food on the island is much more varied than you might expect, encompassing everything from the

rich and complex to grilled simplicity. I've had a lentil salad with the perfect bread and olive spread, lobster and fresh fish, fresh vegetables done in so many ways they're meals unto themselves, and pâtés— too many to choose from if you get to the market early."

You might think that the onslaught of cruise ships disgorging thousands of tourists onto the island every day would be problematic for an international superstar seeking a bit of solitude, but according to Tom, "St. Barth's is like many of the islands in that there are plenty of little places to hide out in. If you time your trips into town or to the more beautiful beaches, you can take care of the shopping and errands or the swimming in the hours before the tour boats unload. Then it's back to the rented niche for the afternoon—a restful and calm day indeed."

Over time, Tom has also come to understand the terrible damage a storm can do to an island as small and vulnerable as St. Barth's. "The need for storm protection is evident in the architecture," he says. "And every storm that hits St. Barth's causes changes to the life of the island beyond the damage to the roads or superstructure. It can be very emotional. A business is gone, a facility is destroyed. But the people get on with what needs to be done with an impressive resilience."

Tom Hanks and Chef Gregg Wangard at Loews' Santa Monica Beach Hotel

Eddy's Lentil Salad

Eddy's is a favorite in Gustavia on Barth's, and Eddy himself is probably the most popular featured item there. He greets customers warmly as they settle in for continental fare that's known to be economical, delicious, and loved by vegetarians for a good selection. One of the prettiest Anglican churches in the Caribbean is your marker—Eddy's is just across the street.

Makes 8 servings

SALAD

5 CUPS (1.2 L) WATER

2 ONIONS, CHOPPED

2 CARROTS, CHOPPED

½ TEASPOON (2.5 ML) DRIED THYME + FRESH
    FOR GARNISH

2 CUPS (480 ML) GREEN LENTILS

SALT AND FRESHLY GROUND BLACK PEPPER

DRESSING

1 TEASPOON (5 ML) DIJON MUSTARD

⅓ CUP (80 ML) BALSAMIC VINEGAR

1 TABLESPOON (15 ML) SHERRY VINEGAR

½ CUP (120 ML) PEANUT OIL

SALT AND FRESHLY GROUND BLACK PEPPER

GARNISH

TRIMMED SCALLIONS

SHALLOTS

TO MAKE THE SALAD: Bring 5 cups (1.2 L) of water in a medium saucepan to a boil. Add the onions, carrots, and thyme and return to a boil. Stir in the lentils, then reduce the heat and simmer, uncovered, for about 20 minutes, or until just tender, and drain. Season to taste with the salt and pepper and let cool.

TO MAKE THE DRESSING: In a small bowl, whisk together the mustard, balsamic vinegar, sherry vinegar, and oil. Season to taste with the salt and pepper.

When ready to serve, toss the salad with the dressing and garnish with the thyme, scallions, and shallots.

OCEAN AND VINE RESTAURANT
LOEWS' SANTA MONICA BEACH HOTEL

Santa Monica, California

Gregg Wangard, Executive Chef

It was a circuitous route via the Caribbean that took Chef Gregg Wangard from his native Wisconsin to his current position as executive chef at the Ocean and Vine Restaurant in Loews' Santa Monica Beach Hotel. As a boy, he learned to appreciate the quality and flavor of farm-fresh ingredients in his grandmother's kitchen; later, he moved on to a 3-year American Culinary Federation accredited apprenticeship and started culinary arts classes at Waukesha Technical College in Wisconsin. From there, at the tender age of 19, he was about to head for another apprenticeship in Florida when Hans Schadler, then executive chef at the Rosewood Caneel Bay Resort on St. John, recognized his talent. Gregg became a chef-in-training at Caneel Bay and for the next 6 months learned to handle the pressures of being a line cook at a busy resort as he began to master the many varieties of Caribbean cuisine. For example, he says, "There are so many different kinds of johnnycakes and conch stew—foods that use the same basic ingredients but have a distinctive regional flair that makes each one 'the best you've ever tasted.'"

One serendipitous result of Gregg's Caribbean adventure was meeting his wife, Kelly, who was working on the line a few stations down from his.

"As you would imagine," Gregg says, "it was really fun to fall in love on St. John. The beauty of the island is so intense and the people so kind. I could go back today and not miss a beat. There is hardly a friendlier place on Earth than St. John and the other Caribbean islands."

The Loews' Hotel in Santa Monica is just a short stint from Tom Hanks's production offices. With its stunning atrium and beachfront views, the hotel is used to accommodating stars—it's hosted many a press junket and celebrity-studded affair—and Chef Gregg happily agreed to re-create Tom's favorite Lentil Salad dish from Eddy's on Barth's for our photo shoot there. Chef Gregg's love for the Caribbean is well-known among his loved ones and admirers. The time he spent there as a younger chef, learning the ropes he now lassos with skill to create sumptuous dishes at this big-city venue, was truly special, and he holds a most cherished place in his heart for the people of the islands.

Conch Fritters with Chipotle Aioli

OCEAN AND VINE RESTAURANT, EXECUTIVE CHEF GREGG WANGARD

Makes 36 fritters and 1¼ cups (300 ml) aioli

AIOLI

1 CUP (240 ML) MAYONNAISE

3 CHIPOTLE PEPPERS IN ADOBO SAUCE, DRAINED
   AND MINCED

JUICE OF 1 LIME

SALT

FRITTERS

1 TABLESPOON (15 ML) VEGETABLE OIL + MORE
   FOR FRYING

½ POUND (227 G) CONCH MEAT, CLEANED,
   COOKED, AND DICED

¼ CUP (60 ML) DICED YELLOW ONION

2 TABLESPOONS (30 ML) MINCED GARLIC

3 EGGS

1½ CUPS (360 ML) MILK

2 TABLESPOONS (30 ML) BAKING POWDER

1 TEASPOON (5 ML) SALT

3 CUPS (720 ML) ALL-PURPOSE FLOUR

1 TABLESPOON (15 ML) CHOPPED FRESH PARSLEY

TO MAKE THE AIOLI: In a small bowl, combine the mayonnaise, peppers, lime juice, and salt to taste. Refrigerate until ready to serve.

TO MAKE THE FRITTERS: Heat the 1 tablespoon (15 ml) oil in a small skillet. Add the conch, onion, and garlic and sauté for about 2 minutes, or until the onion is translucent. Remove from the heat and let cool.

In a large bowl, combine the eggs, milk, baking powder, and salt. Add the flour in three increments, beating until smooth after each addition. Add the parsley and the conch mixture.

Heat about 2" (5 cm) of vegetable oil to 350°F (180°C) in a large, deep pot. Drop in the batter a heaping tablespoon (15 ml) at a time. When the fritters pop up to the surface, roll them around in the oil until evenly browned. They should take 7 to 10 minutes to cook. Transfer to paper towels to drain.

Serve with the aioli for dipping.

Caneel Bay Tropical Fruit Soup

OCEAN AND VINE RESTAURANT, EXECUTIVE CHEF GREGG WANGARD

Makes 12 servings

2 PASSION FRUITS

2 FRESH VANILLA BEAN PODS

½ CORED PINEAPPLE, COARSELY CHOPPED

1 PAPAYA, PEELED, SEEDED, AND COARSELY
   CHOPPED

1 MANGO, PEELED, SEEDED, AND COARSELY
   CHOPPED

½ CANTALOUPE, PEELED, SEEDED, AND COARSELY
   CHOPPED

3 CUPS (720 ML) CUBED WATERMELON

1 CUP (240 ML) COCONUT MILK

½ CUP (120 ML) CREAM OF COCONUT, SUCH AS
   COCO LOPEZ

1 TEASPOON (5 ML) GROUND NUTMEG

¼ CUP (60 ML) SPICED RUM

Cut the passion fruits in half and scoop the seeds into a strainer over a medium bowl. Press lightly on the seeds with the back of a spoon to release the juice.

Cut the vanilla bean pods in half lengthwise, scrape out the seeds, and discard the pods.

In a food processor, combine half the passion fruit juice and the vanilla seeds. Add half the pineapple, papaya, mango, cantaloupe, watermelon, coconut milk, and coconut cream and process with on/off pulses until smooth. Transfer to a large bowl and repeat with the remaining ingredients. Stir in the nutmeg and rum, then refrigerate until ready to serve.

Citrus-Marinated Wahoo with Island Potato Salad and Mango Relish

OCEAN AND VINE RESTAURANT, EXECUTIVE CHEF GREGG WANGARD

Makes 2 servings

POTATO SALAD

½ POUND (227 G) FINGERLING POTATOES

2 TABLESPOONS (30 ML) MAYONNAISE

2 TABLESPOONS (30 ML) SOUR CREAM

1 TABLESPOON (15 ML) DIJON MUSTARD

1 TEASPOON (5 ML) COARSE MUSTARD

1 RIB CELERY, DICED

1 HARD-COOKED EGG, CHOPPED

¼ CUP (60 ML) DICED RED ONION

¼ TEASPOON (1.2 ML) KOSHER SALT

¼ TEASPOON (1.2 ML) FRESHLY GROUND BLACK
    PEPPER

SALSA

½ CUP (120 ML) DICED PINEAPPLE

1 RIPE MANGO, PEELED, SEEDED, AND DICED
    (ABOUT 1¼ CUPS [300 ML])

¼ CUP (60 ML) SLICED SCALLIONS

¼ CUP (60 ML) DICED, SEEDED RED BELL PEPPER

¼ CUP (60 ML) MINCED RED ONION

3 TABLESPOONS (45 ML) LIME JUICE

3 TABLESPOONS (45 ML) PINEAPPLE JUICE

FISH

JUICE OF 1 ORANGE

JUICE OF 1 LIME

½ TEASPOON (2.5 ML) CAYENNE PEPPER

½ TEASPOON (2.5 ML) SWEET PAPRIKA

½ TEASPOON (2.5 ML) CHILI POWDER

2 WAHOO FILLETS, 8 OUNCES (227 G) EACH

SALT

1 TABLESPOON (15 ML) VEGETABLE OIL

(CONTINUED)

TO MAKE THE POTATO SALAD: Bring a large saucepan of water to a boil and cook the potatoes for 15 to 20 minutes, or until tender. Drain and refrigerate until cold.

In a small bowl, whisk together the mayonnaise, sour cream, Dijon mustard, and coarse mustard. Add the celery, egg, and onion and season to taste with the salt and pepper. Peel and cube the cooled potatoes, then add to the mayonnaise mixture and toss gently to combine. Refrigerate until ready to serve.

TO MAKE THE SALSA: In a small bowl, combine the pineapple, mango, scallions, red pepper, onion, lime juice, and pineapple juice. Toss to combine.

TO MAKE THE FISH: In a bowl large enough to hold the fish, combine the orange juice, lime juice, cayenne, paprika, and chili powder. Add the fish and let stand for 30 minutes.

Remove the fish from the marinade and season to taste with the salt. Heat the oil in a skillet over medium heat, add the fish, and sear for 2 minutes on each side, depending on thickness. Cook for 8 to 10 minutes, or until opaque. Serve immediately with salsa and potato salad on the side.

Chocolate Port Wine Sorbet

OCEAN AND VINE RESTAURANT, EXECUTIVE CHEF GREGG WANGARD

Makes 8 servings

2 CUPS (480 ML) WATER

¾ CUP (180 ML) SUGAR

½ CUP (120 ML) COCOA POWDER

1 VANILLA BEAN POD, HALVED LENGTHWISE

½ CUP (120 ML) PORT WINE

4 OUNCES (113 G) BITTERSWEET CHOCOLATE, COARSELY CHOPPED

In a medium saucepan, combine 2 cups (480 ml) water and the sugar, cocoa powder, vanilla bean, and wine. Bring to a boil, then reduce the heat and add the chocolate, stirring just until combined. Remove from the heat and strain. Place the bowl into a larger bowl filled with ice, and stir every 10 minutes until cool. Freeze in an ice cream maker according to the manufacturer's directions.

ST. MAARTEN

TEMPTATION RESTAURANT,
ATLANTIS CASINO IN
THE DUTCH LOWLANDS

Cupecoy, St. Maarten

Dino Jagtiani, Owner/Chef

Sometimes the name of a restaurant says it all, and temptation is definitely where Executive Chef Dino Jagtiani leads diners each night. Chef Dino is the culinary force behind Temptation, the award-winning nouveau Caribbean restaurant at the Atlantis Casino in the Dutch Lowlands on St. Maarten. He is also the first native of the island to have graduated from the prestigious Culinary Institute of America in New York.

After graduation, he joined the Le Meridian and Waldorf organization and spent 2 years in London working at their 4- and 5-star properties. Then came a stint in New York City, trailing some of the best chefs in Manhattan.

At Temptation, Dino now finds new ways to reinterpret those experiences with a menu that reflects travel abroad. Described by some as a taste of SoHo in the Caribbean, the restaurant exudes a big-city atmosphere, complete with a martini bar and jazz piano player, while at the same time staying true to its Caribbean roots.

"For me, nouveau Caribbean cuisine is more about fusing ideas and philosophies than it is about ingredients," explains Chef Dino. "We may combine the artistry and refinement of French food with what a Caribbean grandmother would prepare. For example, if I am preparing Veal Osso Buco, which most people don't consider very Caribbean, I will pair it with a corn polenta that is traditionally served all over the islands. Island recipes are very assertive and bold, and that's how we prepare our meals at Temptation. We also approach our cuisine with a kind of freestyle attitude, with menu items that include everything from tuna tartare to chicken curry, and we like to change it around from month to month. I get such a rush from seeing the nods of approval and gleam of appreciation in my customers' eyes when they take the first bite."

Tempura Mussel Shooters
with Coconut-Cashew Curry and Wakame

TEMPTATION RESTAURANT, CHEF DINO JAGTIANI

There will be curry left over. It's delicious on grilled chicken or fish with a squeeze of lime.

Makes 4 appetizer servings

CURRY

¼ CUP (60 ML) CASHEW NUTS

1 CUP (240 ML) WATER

3 TABLESPOONS (45 ML) OLIVE OIL

¼ ONION, DICED

½ TOMATO, PEELED, SEEDED, AND DICED

½ TEASPOON (2.5 ML) MINCED GINGER

½ TEASPOON (2.5 ML) MINCED GARLIC

½ TEASPOON (2.5 ML) GROUND TURMERIC

½ TEASPOON (2.5 ML) GROUND CORIANDER

½ TEASPOON (2.5 ML) GROUND CUMIN

½ TEASPOON (2.5 ML) CHILI POWDER

½ TEASPOON (2.5 ML) GARAM MASALA

SALT AND FRESHLY GROUND BLACK PEPPER

½ TEASPOON (2.5 ML) MUSTARD SEED

½ CUP (120 ML) COCONUT MILK

TEMPURA

VEGETABLE OIL, FOR FRYING

1 CUP (240 ML) RICE FLOUR

¾ CUP (180 ML) COLD CLUB SODA

20 AUSTRALIAN GREEN LIP MUSSELS, SPLIT OPEN, MEAT REMOVED FROM SHELLS, AND SHELLS RESERVED

1 CUP (240 ML) WAKAME SALAD (SEE RESOURCES, PAGE 247)

TO MAKE THE CURRY: In a small saucepan, simmer the cashews in 1 cup (240 ml) water for about 15 minutes, or until tender. Drain, reserving ½ cup (120 ml) of cooking liquid.

Heat 1 tablespoon (15 ml) of the oil in a medium skillet over medium-high heat. Add the onion, tomato, ginger, garlic, and cashews and cook for about 5 minutes, or until tender. Add the turmeric, coriander, cumin, chili powder, and garam masala and cook for about 1 minute, or until fragrant. Add the reserved cooking liquid, reduce the heat to low, and simmer for 5 minutes. Season to taste with the salt and pepper. Remove from the heat and let cool, then transfer to a small food processor and process until smooth.

(CONTINUED)

Meanwhile, wipe out the skillet and heat the remaining 2 tablespoons (30 ml) oil over medium-high heat. Add the mustard seed and cook for about 1 minute, or until the seeds pop. Return the curry to the pan, stir in the coconut milk, and season to taste with the salt and pepper. Remove from the heat and keep warm.

TO MAKE THE TEMPURA: In a large, deep pot, heat 2" (5 cm) of oil to 350°F (180°C).

In a small bowl, combine the rice flour and club soda to make a batter (it should be the consistency of thin pancake batter). Dip the mussels into the batter, then fry for 1 minute, or until crisp and golden. Transfer to paper towels to drain.

TO ASSEMBLE THE SHOOTERS: Fill each half shell with about 1 teaspoon (5 ml) curry sauce. Place a mussel in each shell and top with some of the Wakame Salad.

McDino's Apple Pie

TEMPTATION RESTAURANT, CHEF DINO JAGTIANI

Makes 8 servings

VEGETABLE OIL, FOR FRYING

1 CUP (240 ML) RICE FLOUR

1 CUP (240 ML) COLD GINGER ALE OR SELTZER
WATER

4 GRANNY SMITH APPLES, PEELED, CORED, AND
QUARTERED

¾ CUP (180 ML) CONFECTIONERS' SUGAR

½ CUP (120 ML) PREPARED CARAMEL SAUCE

5 SPRIGS FRESH THYME, MINCED

VANILLA ICE CREAM

In a large, deep pot or skillet, heat 1" (2.5 cm) of oil to 350°F (180°C).

In a large bowl, combine the flour and ginger ale to make a batter (it should be the consistency of thin pancake batter, so add more ginger ale if necessary). Coat the apples with the batter, slip them into the oil, and fry, turning as necessary, for 4 to 5 minutes, or until crisp and golden. Using a slotted spoon, remove the apples from the oil. Drain on paper towels.

Arrange 2 apple quarters on each plate, sift confectioners' sugar over the apples, drizzle with the caramel sauce, sprinkle with the thyme, and place a scoop of ice cream on the side. Serve warm.

NEVIS

FOUR SEASONS RESORT

Charlestown, Nevis

Cyrille Pannier, Executive Chef

"I've always been into food—mostly eating when I was a kid," Chef Cyrille Pannier jokes. "But eating is training, too, when you live in Le Mans." On this point, he is quite serious. Situated in the Loire Valley, Le Mans is home not only to one of the world's great automobile races but also to some of the finest French food and wine.

"The French training is very classical. The peeling of onions, the slicing of carrots—all are done to a standard. For 3 years, I studied in the restaurants and hotels of St. Tropez, Paris, and Biarritz as well as Le Mans. Then, about 7 years ago, my work brought me to Palm Beach, where I began to experiment with exotic foods and fish.

"After 4 years there, I was offered my current position on Nevis. I had discovered diving in Florida and had become certified, so the opportunity to live on an island was ideal. The sand and the colors that surround you in the water are unbelievable, and the silence is mind-boggling. The marine life—from sharks to turtles and stingrays—swimming with you as if you were a fish. It's magical."

Now, once a week, guests of the Four Seasons Resort join Chef Cyrille in an interactive dining experience called "Dive and Dine." "First, we dive. Then the guests relax on the beach as we prepare the food, and we eat together while we talk about the dive.

"The bounty from each dive varies, but one item the guests always clamor for is lobster. Luckily, in Nevis it is plentiful. We have shoe lobsters, which hide under the sand and are difficult to spot. The locals catch them by putting food in a trap. But we also have the spiny lobster, which is the most popular and abundant.

"Three different endangered species of turtle sometimes swim with us on our dives, as do the local fish—the wahoo, the mahi mahi, and the multicolored reef fish. I love cooking on the beach with the smell of the sea and the grill. We start right around sunset, when the stars are in front of you. That's magical, too."

But Chef Cyrille also knows that sometimes island living isn't so magical. "The people of Nevis and the other islands know what it is to live with storms like the one that hit Grenada. This island sent dry food and clothing to Grenada. The resort and other organizations held drives; locals donated food and cash. Everyone helped because it is necessary. Anyone who lives on an island knows how hard it is to survive in poststorm conditions. The bananas, coconuts, peanuts, and sugarcane we use in our cooking all came from Grenada. It will take years to rejuvenate the land to create the quality crops they had before the storm."

Black Antiguan Pineapple with Montgay Rum and Vanilla Sauce and Soursop Sorbet

FOUR SEASONS RESORT, NEVIS, EXECUTIVE CHEF CYRILLE PANNIER

The black pineapple, from Antigua, is smaller than what's found in the States and has an intense, sweet flavor. If you can't find it, substitute a small, ripe, regular pineapple.

Makes 4 servings

3 TABLESPOONS (45 ML) BUTTER, CUT INTO
   SMALL PIECES

1 RIPE PINEAPPLE, PEELED AND CORED AND CUT
   INTO 8 SLICES (¾" [1.9 CM] EACH)

½ CUP (120 ML) LIGHT BROWN SUGAR

MONTGAY RUM AND VANILLA SAUCE (RECIPE
   FOLLOWS)

SOURSOP SORBET (RECIPE FOLLOWS)

In a large skillet over medium heat, melt the butter. Add the pineapple and sauté until the slices are golden in color, for 10 to 15 minutes. Remove to a baking sheet and sprinkle with brown sugar while still hot. Spoon equal amounts of vanilla sauce on each of 4 plates, then arrange 2 pineapple slices in the center of each plate and spoon equal amounts of sorbet on the side.

MONTGAY RUM AND VANILLA SAUCE

1 CUP (240 ML) MILK

1 CUP (240 ML) HEAVY CREAM

½ CUP (120 ML) SUGAR

1 VANILLA BEAN POD, HALVED

5 EGG YOLKS

2 TABLESPOONS (30 ML) MONTGAY RUM

In a medium saucepan, combine the milk, cream, half the sugar, and the vanilla bean and bring to a boil.

In a medium bowl, whisk together the egg yolks and the remaining ¼ cup (60 ml) sugar. Gradually whisk in half the boiled milk. Pour the egg mixture into the pan and cook, stirring constantly, for 3 to 4 minutes, or until thick enough to coat the back of a spoon. Whisk in the rum, transfer to a bowl, and set the bowl into a larger container filled with ice to chill.

SOURSOP SORBET

4 CUPS (1 L) SOURSOP PUREE (SEE RESOURCES, PAGE 247)

2 CUPS (480 ML) SIMPLE SYRUP (SEE NOTE)

In a medium bowl, combine the puree and syrup, then freeze in an ice cream maker according to the manufacturer's directions. You can make the sorbet ahead and refrigerate for up to 5 days.

NOTE: *To make simple syrup, heat equal parts water and sugar over high heat until dissolved.*

Chilled Spiced Coconut Soup

FOUR SEASONS RESORT, NEVIS, EXECUTIVE CHEF CYRILLE PANNIER

Makes 4 servings

2 TABLESPOONS (30 ML) BUTTER

1 MEDIUM WHITE ONION, CHOPPED

2 TABLESPOONS (30 ML) CURRY POWDER

1 CUP (240 ML) CHICKEN STOCK

1 CUP (240 ML) COCONUT MILK

2 TABLESPOONS (30 ML) CRÈME FRAICHE

1 MEDIUM PAPAYA, PEELED, SEEDED, AND DICED

¾ CUP (180 ML) SHREDDED FRESH COCONUT

SALT AND FRESHLY GROUND BLACK PEPPER

COARSELY GRATED COCONUT, TOASTED (SEE NOTE)

Melt the butter in a medium saucepan over medium heat. Add the onion and sauté just until soft but not browned. Reduce the heat to low, add the curry powder, and cook, stirring, for about 3 minutes.

Add the stock, coconut milk, crème fraiche, and papaya and simmer for about 5 minutes. Add the shredded coconut, season to taste with the salt and pepper, and puree with an immersion blender until smooth. Refrigerate for at least 2 hours, then garnish with the toasted coconut before serving.

NOTE: *To toast coconut, preheat the oven to 350°F (180°C). Scatter the coconut on a baking sheet and bake for 3 to 4 minutes, or until golden.*

Grilled Caribbean Lobster with Passion Fruit Glaze and Vegetable Slaw

FOUR SEASONS RESORT, NEVIS, EXECUTIVE CHEF CYRILLE PANNIER

Makes 2 servings

GLAZE

4 LARGE PASSION FRUIT

1 TABLESPOON (15 ML) HONEY

1 TABLESPOON (15 ML) RUM

1 TABLESPOON (15 ML) UNSALTED BUTTER

SLAW

2 TABLESPOONS (30 ML) FISH SAUCE (NOCNAM)

1 TABLESPOON (15 ML) RICE WINE VINEGAR

1 TABLESPOON (15 ML) SUGAR

1 SMALL CARROT, CUT INTO THIN STRIPS

1 SMALL PAPAYA, PEELED, SEEDED, AND CUT INTO THIN STRIPS

1 SMALL RED BELL PEPPER, CORED, SEEDED, AND CUT INTO THIN STRIPS

1 SMALL YELLOW BELL PEPPER, CORED, SEEDED, AND CUT INTO THIN STRIPS

1 SMALL GREEN BELL PEPPER, CORED, SEEDED, AND CUT INTO THIN STRIPS

1 TABLESPOON (15 ML) CHOPPED FRESH CILANTRO

LOBSTER

1 MEDIUM CARIBBEAN SPINY LOBSTER

SALT AND FRESHLY GROUND BLACK PEPPER

OLIVE OIL

TO MAKE THE GLAZE: Halve the passion fruit, scoop the seeds into a strainer over a clean bowl, and press lightly with the back of a spoon to release the juice. In a small saucepan over medium-high heat, combine the juice, honey, rum, and butter. Bring to a boil and cook for 1 minute, then remove from the heat. (The glaze can be refrigerated for up to 1 week.)

TO MAKE THE SLAW: In a large bowl, combine the fish sauce, vinegar, and sugar. Add the carrot, papaya, bell peppers, and cilantro and toss gently to combine.

TO MAKE THE LOBSTER: Preheat the grill on high heat. Using a large chef's knife, split the lobster in half lengthwise. Clean the cavity, then rinse well and pat dry. Season the cavity to taste with the salt and pepper, drizzle with the oil, and grill for approximately 10 minutes, or until the meat is opaque. Brush with the glaze and grill for 3 minutes. Arrange each half on a plate topped with the slaw.

ANTIGUA

THE HOME RESTAURANT

Gambles Terrace, Antigua

Carl and Rita Thomas, Owners

When Carl Thomas returned to Antigua in 1991 after working for more than 2 decades in the New York culinary world, he knew he'd truly come home. In Manhattan, fellow chefs had constantly encouraged Chef Carl to open his own restaurant, so when he and his wife, Rita, returned to his boyhood home in Antigua, the name of his venture—The Home Restaurant—was an easy choice.

"My objective was to allow guests to experience the Caribbean that I had known as a boy through a unique food experience," explains Chef Carl, who is executive chef and co-owner of the restaurant. "Everything is made here at the restaurant, including our breads and desserts."

Claiming that he grows bored preparing the same dishes year after year, Chef Carl loves to "mix it up" but still has several favorites that have been on the menu since the Home Restaurant opened in 1992. This includes an amazing and sinfully rich bread pudding, which came about in a most interesting way. "I was in a Pier 1 store in the States in 1991 and bought a gigantic glass jar with a cork top and a big, open, wide mouth," says Chef Carl. "I filled it up with fruit as soon as I returned to the island, and it has never been empty since. The fruit, which includes figs, raisins, cherries, and whatever else sounds delicious at the time, is what comprises the base of our ever-changing bread pudding. This concoction is laced with Cognac, sherry, and port wine and served over the stiff pudding."

Another favorite at the restaurant is Chicken and Shrimp in a Pineapple Pontoon, which is prepared with a blend of island flavors, including fresh ginger, lemon peel, cilantro, chili paste, and basil. "It sounds complex but is really very easy."

Antiguan Bread Pudding

THE HOME RESTAURANT, CHEF CARL THOMAS

Makes 8 servings

PUDDING

9 SLICES WHITE BREAD

1¾ CUPS (420 ML) WHOLE MILK

¾ CUP (180 ML) BROWN SUGAR

4 TABLESPOONS (60 ML) UNSALTED BUTTER

1 CUP (240 ML) YELLOW RAISINS

¾ CUP (180 ML) PORT WINE OR BURGUNDY

5 EGGS

½ CUP (120 ML) HEAVY CREAM

1 TEASPOON (5 ML) GROUND NUTMEG

1 TEASPOON (5 ML) GROUND CINNAMON

1 TEASPOON (5 ML) GROUND GINGER

1 TEASPOON (5 ML) VANILLA EXTRACT

1 TEASPOON (5 ML) ALMOND EXTRACT

SAUCE

4 TABLESPOONS (60 ML) BUTTER

1 CUP (240 ML) BROWN SUGAR

1 TEASPOON (5 ML) VANILLA EXTRACT

¼ CUP (60 ML) DARK RUM

1 CUP (240 ML) HEAVY CREAM
OR HALF-AND-HALF

Grease a 13" x 9" (32.5 x 23 cm) baking dish and preheat the oven to 375°F (190°C).

TO MAKE THE PUDDING: Cut the bread into 1" (2.5 cm) cubes and arrange in a single layer on a baking sheet. Toast for about 5 minutes, or until golden. Leave the oven set at 375°F (190°C).

In a medium saucepan over medium heat, combine the milk, sugar, and butter and cook for 4 minutes.

In a bowl, soak the raisins in the port wine or burgundy for 5 minutes.

In another large bowl, whisk together the eggs, cream, nutmeg, cinnamon, ginger, vanilla extract, and almond extract until thoroughly combined. Add the milk mixture, raisins, and bread cubes and fold gently to combine. Pour into the prepared pan and bake for 45 minutes.

TO MAKE THE SAUCE: In a medium saucepan over low heat, combine the butter and sugar and cook just until the sugar melts and turns golden, being careful not to let it burn. Add the vanilla extract and remove from the heat. Stir in the rum and cream or half-and-half, return to the heat, and cook for 10 minutes, until slightly thickened.

Cut the pudding into individual portions and pour the sauce over the top.

ANTIGUA

Chicken and Shrimp in a Pineapple Pontoon

THE HOME RESTAURANT, CHEF CARL THOMAS

Makes 6 servings

SAUCE

1 TABLESPOON (15 ML) OLIVE OIL

1 LARGE ONION, CHOPPED

1 RED BELL PEPPER, CORED, SEEDED, AND CHOPPED

1 TEASPOON (5 ML) FINELY CHOPPED GARLIC

1 CUP (240 ML) CHOPPED FRESH CILANTRO

1 CUP (240 ML) CHOPPED FRESH BASIL

2 TEASPOONS (10 ML) DARK BROWN SUGAR

4 TABLESPOONS (60 ML) SOY SAUCE

2 TEASPOONS (10 ML) GRATED FRESH GINGER

1 TEASPOON (5 ML) CHILI PASTE

1 TEASPOON (5 ML) TAMARIND PASTE

2 TABLESPOONS (30 ML) CORNSTARCH DISSOLVED IN 1 CUP (240 ML) WATER

CHICKEN AND SHRIMP

3 MEDIUM PINEAPPLES

1 CUP (240 ML) ALL-PURPOSE FLOUR

1 CUP (240 ML) CORNSTARCH

SALT AND FRESHLY GROUND BLACK PEPPER

4 (6 OUNCES [170 G] EACH) BONELESS, SKINLESS CHICKEN BREAST HALVES

3 POUNDS (1.4 KG) LARGE SHRIMP, DEVEINED AND TAILS REMOVED

¼ CUP (60 ML) OLIVE OIL

½ TEASPOON (2.5 ML) GRATED ORANGE ZEST

2 STAR ANISE

TO MAKE THE SAUCE: Heat the oil in a large skillet over medium heat. Add the onion, bell pepper, and garlic and cook for about 5 minutes, or until the onion is translucent. Increase the heat to high, add the cilantro and basil, and cook for 2 minutes.

Add the brown sugar, soy sauce, ginger, chili paste, and tamarind paste. Reduce the heat, add the cornstarch mixture, and stir for 1 minute. Remove from the heat, cover, and keep warm.

TO MAKE THE CHICKEN AND SHRIMP: Cut the pineapples in half lengthwise and remove the flesh with a paring knife, being careful to leave the shells intact. Cut the fruit into small chunks and set aside along with the shells.

(CONTINUED)

CHICKEN AND SHRIMP IN A PINEAPPLE PONTOON-CONTINUED

In a bowl, combine the flour and cornstarch and season with a pinch of the salt and pepper. Cut the chicken breasts into 1" (2.5 cm) pieces, pat dry, and season to taste with salt and pepper. Toss the chicken in the flour mixture and set aside on a plate. Toss the shrimp in the flour mixture and set aside on a separate plate.

Heat the oil in a large skillet over medium heat. Add the orange zest and star anise. Increase the heat to medium-high, add the chicken, and cook, turning occasionally, for 10 to 12 minutes, or until golden on all sides and no longer pink in the middle.

Transfer the chicken to a large bowl and add the shrimp to the skillet. Cook, turning occasionally, for 10 to 12 minutes, or until pink. If any oil remains in the skillet, transfer the shrimp to the bowl with the chicken and drain off the oil. Return the skillet to the stove and reduce the heat to medium. Add the sauce, chicken, and shrimp and cook, stirring gently, for about 1 minute, or until warmed through.

TO ASSEMBLE THE DISH: Arrange one pineapple shell on each plate, fill with the chicken and shrimp, and top with the pineapple chunks.

DOMINICA

Orlando Bloom

An Adventurer's Paradise

Orlando Jonathan Blanchard Bloom is known the world over for his substantial talent and extraordinary good looks. As a child, the actor struggled with dyslexia before winning a scholarship that would take him to the British American Drama Academy and later the Guildhall School of Music and Drama. A serious fall while he was still in school left him with a broken back, and it was feared that he would never walk again. But Orlando's perseverance and good-natured outlook helped bring him through the worst to a full recovery.

After acting in a handful of films and British television programs, he landed his first major movie role, playing the beloved elf Legolas in the *Lord of the Rings* trilogy. But it was his turn as the dashing Will Turner in *Pirates of the Caribbean: The Curse of the Black Pearl*—the blockbuster first film in the Disney series—and in its sequel, *Pirates of the Caribbean: Dead Man's Chest,* that he definitively earned star status and discovered the islands' many wonders, which include the wonderful food of Dominica.

His role in the *Pirates* series has inadvertently made Mr. Bloom something of a connoisseur of Caribbean cuisine; after all, he's filmed in and around several of the islands of the strip to make the three films in the hugely successful franchise. "We've had an interesting time in the Caribbean, but Dominica has had the most impact on me and the crew," Orlando says, speaking like the adventurer you would expect him to be about an island whose offerings for tourists don't include star-rated resort amenities or even a variety of restaurants. "Bananas are the chief export," notes Orlando, "and ecotourism is really the main revenue for Dominica. It's a very poor island but very beautiful."

"I love fish and red meat and chicken—I eat whatever's going," he says. "The fruit was amazing, particularly the guava. While we were shooting *Pirates,* craft services, who supplied our meals, would cut up the local fruit and mix it into whatever they were serving that day. Guava on Dominica, coconuts on St. Vincent's—when the fruit changed, it was another indicator that the production had moved to a new location."

Dominica was just right for filming, and a couple of places were also just right for eating—one, in particular, for Orlando. "We found this place called Indigo that's run by Marie Frederick and her husband, Clem. It's an amazing tree house—really off the beaten path. You travel down a wobbly path to find this little Robinson Crusoe scene. Signs dotted throughout the place say things like, 'No photos—beauty is for now.' " And that sentiment is most eloquently displayed in Marie Frederick's cooking, which is offered to a small number of guests at the rustic bed and breakfast whose wood-fired stove does most of its work on an exterior landing.

In her thick, warm French accent, Marie begins, "I'd lived for some time in St. Maarten and Anguilla, and a friend who was captain of a banana boat brought me here on vacation. When I first came to the Caribbean, I had no idea about Dominica, but when I arrived here in 1988, I fell in love immediately. To me it looked like the Garden of Eden."

Not long after that, Marie returned for good. "One Friday night, I was out at a discothèque on the beach and I met this Rastafarian," she chuckles. "The rest is history." Clem, a natural citizen of

the island, is from a village called Borne, near Portsmith. Clem and Marie were married on St. Lucia in 1991 and have a son, Isaiah.

Clem is responsible for creating much of the artwork and precious mottos that are on display and sold at the compound. "There are lots of signs around our place. My husband has many 'words of wisdom' for us to live by. One is 'Nothing makes man happy. Happiness is in the mind.'

"When you are here, it is very secluded. You don't see anything around you but the mountains. We seat only about eight people. The food we cook is island food but vegetarian or Italian-influenced—using organic produce and a lot of fish for protein," Marie says. "I was born in Deauville in Normandy, but my cooking is influenced less by France than by my travels to Greece and Morocco. I cannot live without olive oil. My style is everything fresh—and usually with lots of ginger in it."

Marie is renowned for her warm breads presented simply with a grated fresh ginger garnish. Other favorite dishes of the lucky and select patrons who are privileged to sit at her table include a tomato salad made with fresh basil and mozzarella and served with her famous fresh bread; an intense carrot salad with grated ginger; Pasta au Pistou, cooked al dente and tossed in a smooth homemade paste of garlic, parsley, basil, Parmesan, and olive oil; and heady, aromatic smoked blue marlin soaked in cream and served over penne pasta. "I also serve lots of pasta and pizza," says Marie, "and most dishes come with fresh vegetables from the land.

"Orlando liked the breadfruit very much," she beams. "It's first blackened on the wood fire, then cut and fried into chips." Indigo also makes a particularly delectable breadfruit fritter that's fried in a locally produced coconut oil to make it extra crisp and flavorful. Orlando confesses that the breadfruit was one of his favorites. Breadfruit is loaded with leucine, an essental amino acid, which provides strength to last through an intense shoot or keep up with the array of action sports offered on Dominica.

"I love to swim, and the water was very beautiful and still where I was staying. The sulfur springs and the waterfalls were amazing. Dominica is one of the islands that's most untouched. From the ocean, certain parts look uninhabited and raw," Orlando says. "Certainly, different parts of the Caribbean have become holiday destinations, but Dominica's charm lies in its unrefined nature."

The island environment is protected by the local government and by the Carib Indians, who are considered the oldest culture to inhabit the area. "Some Carib Indians worked on the movie as extras," he says. "We took a boat ride—there's a scene where we go upriver—and passed an old bridge that was being torn down. One of the Carib told me that it had once been a railroad bridge, but when Hurricane David hit in 1979, the railroad, which had originally been built by the British around the turn of the century, was destroyed. Many of the Carib Indians, who were concentrated where the hurricane hit hardest, had to move to the other side of the island."

Slowly but surely, however, the island is being rebuilt, and tourists are returning in greater numbers. "We do have Hollywood stars," says Marie, "but half the time I don't know who they are because we don't have a television. Only if I recognize their faces from magazines do I realize who they are."

Breadfruit Fritters

INDIGO RESTAURANT, CHEF MARIE FREDERICK

Makes 4 servings

1 LARGE BREADFRUIT

COCONUT OIL

SALT

Roast the breadfruit on a grill or over an open flame until the skin is charred. Peel and slice thinly.

Heat 1" (2.5 cm) of oil in a deep skillet. Working in batches, fry the breadfruit until golden on both sides. Transfer to paper towels to drain, and season to taste with the salt.

Pasta, Smoked Fish, and Cream

INDIGO RESTAURANT, CHEF MARIE FREDERICK

Makes 4 to 6 servings

1 PACKET (6 OUNCES [170 G]) SMOKED SALMON
   OR MARLIN

1 CLOVE GARLIC, CRUSHED

¼ CUP (60 ML) OLIVE OIL

SALT AND FRESHLY GROUND BLACK PEPPER

1 CUP (240 ML) HALF-AND-HALF

FRESHLY GRATED PARMESAN CHEESE

1 MEDIUM GREEN PAPAYA, SEEDED AND PEELED

16 OUNCES (454 G) PENNE PASTA, COOKED
   ACCORDING TO PACKAGE DIRECTIONS

HOT PEPPER FLAKES (OPTIONAL)

CHOPPED FRESH CILANTRO

In a medium bowl, combine the salmon or marlin, garlic, and oil. Refrigerate for 2 hours. Drain off the marinade, cut the salmon or marlin into bite-size pieces, and return to the bowl. Season to taste with the salt and black pepper and stir in the half-and-half and Parmesan to taste.

While the salmon is marinating, slice the papaya into bite-size strips and steam until tender. Remove from the heat and let cool.

In a large bowl, gently stir together the pasta, papaya, and salmon or marlin mixture. Sprinkle with the hot pepper, if desired, and garnish with the cilantro.

Pasta au Pistou

INDIGO RESTAURANT, CHEF MARIE FREDERICK

Makes 6 servings

16 OUNCES (454 G) PASTA, SUCH AS FUSILLI OR SPAGHETTI

1 LARGE BUNCH PARSLEY (ABOUT 2 CUPS [480 ML] TRIMMED)

1 CUP (240 ML) FRESH BASIL

4 CLOVES GARLIC

6 TABLESPOONS (90 ML) FRESHLY GRATED PARMESAN CHEESE

½ TEASPOON (2.5 ML) SALT + EXTRA FOR SEASONING

2 TABLESPOONS (30 ML) OLIVE OIL, DIVIDED

1 MEDIUM ONION, CHOPPED

1 CAN (28 OUNCES [793 G]) DICED TOMATOES, DRAINED

1 TABLESPOON (15 ML) BROWN SUGAR

Cook the pasta according to package directions until al dente, then drain and rinse with cold water for 30 seconds. Transfer to a large bowl and keep warm.

In a blender or food processor, combine the parsley, basil, garlic, cheese, salt, and 1 tablespoon (15 ml) of the oil and process until a smooth paste forms.

Heat the remaining 1 tablespoon (15 ml) of oil in a medium skillet over medium heat. Add the onion and cook, stirring occasionally, for about 7 minutes, or until soft. Add the tomatoes and cook for about 5 minutes, or until slightly thickened. Reduce the heat to medium-low and season to taste with the salt. Add the brown sugar and cook for 5 to 7 minutes, or until thick. Remove from the heat and stir in the herb mixture. Toss the pasta with the sauce and serve immediately.

Chocolate Delight

INDIGO RESTAURANT, CHEF MARIE FREDERICK

Makes 8 servings

¼ CUP (60 ML) HOT BLACK COFFEE

1 STICK CINNAMON OR ½ TEASPOON (2.5 ML) GROUND CINNAMON

⅓ CUP (80 ML) COCOA POWDER

1 CUP (240 ML) GRANULATED SUGAR

¼ CUP (60 ML) BUTTER

½ CUP (120 ML) MILK

½ TEASPOON (2.5 ML) VANILLA EXTRACT

PINCH OF GROUND NUTMEG

1½ TEASPOONS (7.5 ML) GRATED FRESH GINGER OR ½ TEASPOON (2.5 ML) GROUND GINGER

1 EGG

1¼ CUPS (300 ML) ALL-PURPOSE FLOUR

½ TEASPOON (2.5 ML) BAKING POWDER

½ TEASPOON (2.5 ML) BAKING SODA

CONFECTIONERS' SUGAR

GINGER OR COCONUT ICE CREAM (OPTIONAL)

Preheat the oven to 350°F (180°C). Coat a 9" (23 cm) cake pan with nonstick cooking spray.

Place the coffee in a small bowl, add the cinnamon sticks or ground cinnamon, and let stand for 10 minutes. Add the cocoa, and when it dissolves, remove the cinnamon stick.

In a medium bowl, cream the sugar and butter. One at a time, add the milk, vanilla extract, nutmeg, ginger, and egg, stirring well after each addition. Add the cocoa mixture and stir. Add the flour, baking powder, and baking soda and stir just until combined. Pour into the prepared pan and bake for 30 to 35 minutes. Let cool for 10 minutes, then remove from the pan and let cool completely. Dust with the confectioners' sugar and serve with the ice cream, if desired.

MUSTIQUE

Alfre Woodard

FROM OUR HOME TO THEIR HOME

Award-winning performer Alfre Woodard broke into the acting scene in 1983 in a big way when she was nominated for an Academy Award for her performance as Geechee in the movie *Cross Creek*. Alternating between television and films with amazing range and versatility, Alfre's next professional milestones came in the mid-1980s, when she won Emmy Awards for recurring roles on *LA Law* and *Hill Street Blues*.

Constantly pursuing challenging and unconventional roles, Ms. Woodard received a Golden Globe nomination for her role in John Sayles's *Passion Fish* and the Triple Crown of American television honors—an Emmy, a Golden Globe, and a Screen Actors Guild Award—for her performance in the lead role in the HBO film *Miss Evers' Boys*.

Over the past 4 years, she has switched back and forth seamlessly between comedy and drama, costarring in *Radio* with Cuba Gooding Jr., *The Forgotten* with Julianne Moore, *Beauty Shop* with Queen Latifah, and *Take the Lead* with Antonio Banderas. And as a total change of pace, Alfre joined the cast of ABC's hit series *Desperate Housewives* as the eccentric Betty Applewhite for the 2005/2006 season.

Alfre's travel philosophy is simple—her best times are to be had when she physically and spiritually leaves her Los Angeles home and seeks relaxation and rejuvenation. She experiences this feeling in the southernmost reaches of the Caribbean where, when traveling by boat, she is able to slow down her hectic life and truly connect with the islands and their people.

One of Alfre Woodard's most memorable Caribbean getaways was a 10-day sailing trip she and her husband, Roderick Spencer, took from petite St. Vincent south to the Grenadines, stopping at beautiful remote ports such as Canouan Island, Union Island, Mustique, and even some private cays.

When she takes the time to vacation, Alfre really likes to get away from the hustle and bustle of city life and enjoy a completely different environment and culture. Sailing to the southernmost reaches of the Caribbean, away from the 5-star luxury resorts and US territories, gives her the kind of experience that truly replenishes her soul. "When I leave home, I want to visit someone else's home," she explains. "I still felt like I was in the mix on St. Lucia, which is a remarkably beautiful island with rugged terrain, but it still has big cities with lots of nightlife. My prescription for slowing down and decompressing is getting on a boat and taking daytrips where there is no interruption between you, the people, and the water."

Alfre has great respect for the island people, whom she believes to have a practicality that derives naturally from living a much slower and efficient life than we are used to and from learning to exist very well with what they have. "I'm never as wasteful in the Caribbean as in California, even though I feel that I live a pretty ecological life. It's always enlightening, and I bring that spirit back with me." In addition to helping her slow down, traveling by boat, where space is at a premium, has made Alfre realize that she truly doesn't need so much "stuff."

But not all of Alfre's adventures were learning experiences. One that was just pure fun took place on Mustique, the island where such notables as rock legend Mick Jagger and sportswear mogul Tommy Hilfiger own homes. They dropped anchor in the evening, and after a visit to Basil's Bar, her husband, Roderick, their captain, and the cook they'd hired for the journey decided to prepare an onboard barbecue. Several rum cocktails later, the cook put a loin of pork marinated with rum, garlic, and molasses on the grill.

"It was succulent and moist on the inside and crispy on the outside," says Alfre, "but after biting into it, one of the four of us decided we needed some Grey Poupon mustard, and of course, we didn't have any on board. I informed Roderick and our skipper that we didn't have any Poupon in the kitchen and let them know that it was 9 o'clock at night and there were no stores open. You could

hear laughter from the other boats and smell all these great food aromas coming from the island, and I was perfectly content to dine on my pork without Poupon.

"But the guys were adamant and decided to go up to Prince's End—you can imagine what kinds of homes are located there—and ask someone if they could borrow some Grey Poupon! I said, 'No, you can't do that. Those people have come here to get away from it all.' I had visions of Roderick and our skipper being wrestled to the ground for trespassing, so I unleashed the dinghy, which meant they couldn't get to shore. The next morning, I told Roderick I'd saved them both from being jailed on Mustique, but he still felt that if he'd been able to ring the bell, some cool islander would have understood that if you run out of mustard, you can certainly borrow some from your neighbor. Personally, I wasn't willing to risk it on that island!"

On Jamaica, however, where she and Roderick have also spent time, Alfre believes that he could very easily have borrowed Grey Poupon.

She loves visiting the Hopewell area of the island and staying in Round Hill, which boasts some very low-key and elegant resorts that are not as well known to tourists. And true to her vision of traveling to visit someone else's home, when they're there, she and her traveling companions spend time with the islanders who work at the resorts and live in Hopewell, or they travel up to Mayfield Falls, which is tucked into the mountains, to visit with some "Rastafarian brothers."

"My son has dreadlocks. I don't think that he has ever had his hair combed," says Alfre. "He has been visiting Mayfield since he was 10 months old, and I can remember his telling me when he was a young boy that he wanted to grow his dreadlocks down to his knees 'like the brothers.' It was so cool for him to see a reflection of himself and the way he looked even though it was in a different country. The experience makes me feel good to be among men."

For 11 years, a Jamaican woman traveled with Alfre and helped to raise her children. Most important, however, she embodied the values that are so important to the actress and her family. One meal that "Auntie Annette" invented and prepared for them was a fragrant shrimp dish made with garlic, ginger, jerk seasoning, curry powder, and coconut milk and served with plantains and jasmine rice. Other Caribbean favorites that tickle Alfre's palate include the escovitch and festival bread that are always served at holidays, especially during the Christmas and Easter seasons.

"The main thing I love about island cuisine is that the taste starts as soon as you put it into your mouth," Alfre says. "You have one flavor initially, and because the food is cooked with so many different spices, the taste changes as you eat. I don't like food that is afraid to be seasoned—the bolder the better. Recipes are the safest route, but I always add more spices as long as they don't overwhelm the dish. Truly fine Caribbean cuisine demands a long mealtime. You have to enjoy the different tastes along with great conversation and good music."

This Caribbean boldness of flavor is also evident in the people and culture that have become so important to Alfre. "There is a unique spirit in the Caribbean, and its people are the living monuments," she explains. "Each island and port we stopped at had a very different feel, and I'm not talking about the landscape. Their differences lie in the people—from what they're talking about and how they're saying it to their laughter and celebrations. Although their spices and cooking may be similar, each place we visited had a different way of shaking them up to create a very distinct flavor and taste. I love to listen to the people talk about what they're cooking and how they're preparing these wonderful dishes.

"There is a common feel throughout the various islands, but if you slow down enough, you can see and appreciate what makes each location unique. You can visit the Caribbean every few months for an entire lifetime, and there will still be some new place to discover as the more familiar places start to feel like home."

Escovitch Fish

ALFRE WOODARD AND RODERICK SPENCER

Escovitch Fish is a very popular dish that's prepared throughout the Caribbean, usually served with bammy (cake made from cassava root) or festival bread. Escovitch Fish is served in many homes during the Easter holiday, as a tradition in observance of Lent.

Makes 4 servings

2 POUNDS (1 KG) RED SNAPPER, CUT INTO
    1" (2.5 CM)-THICK SLICES

JUICE OF 1 LEMON OR LIME

1 TABLESPOON (15 ML) SALT

1½ TABLESPOONS (22.5 ML) FRESHLY GROUND
    BLACK PEPPER

2 TABLESPOONS (30 ML) GARLIC POWDER

1 TABLESPOON (15 ML) DRIED JERK SEASONING
    (OPTIONAL)

¼ CUP (60 ML) VEGETABLE OIL

1 LARGE ONION, SLICED

½ RED BELL PEPPER, CORED, SEEDED, AND CUT
    INTO CIRCLES

½ GREEN BELL PEPPER, CORED, SEEDED, AND CUT
    INTO CIRCLES

⅓ CUP (80 ML) THINLY SLICED CARROTS

1⅓ CUPS (320 ML) WHITE CANE VINEGAR
    (SEE RESOURCES, PAGE 245)

½ TEASPOON (2.5 ML) GROUND ALLSPICE

Wash and dry the fish, then rub with the lemon or lime juice. In a small bowl, combine the salt, pepper, garlic powder, and jerk seasoning, if desired, in a small bowl. Pat the fish dry with paper towels, then coat thoroughly with the seasonings.

Heat the oil in a large, deep skillet over medium-high heat. Add the fish and fry for about 5 minutes on each side, or until crisp and brown. Transfer to a deep serving dish and set aside.

Drain all but 2 tablespoons (30 ml) oil from the skillet, return to the heat, and add the onion, bell peppers, carrots, vinegar, and allspice. Bring to a boil, then reduce the heat and simmer until the onion is tender. Remove from the heat and pour over the fish. Serve at room temperature.

Sorrel

ALFRE WOODARD AND RODERICK SPENCER

This is a delightful traditional holiday drink in the Caribbean. Sorrel, also called hibiscus, is a rare plant usually found in the Caribbean during December, when daylight is at its shortest. If you can't find sorrel, you can use red zinger tea, which contains hibiscus. You can also increase the amounts of sugar and rum if you wish.

10 CUPS (2.3 L) COLD WATER

1 TABLESPOON (15 ML) RICE

5 TABLESPOONS (75 ML) GRATED FRESH GINGER

½ TEASPOON (2.5 ML) WHOLE CLOVES

12 WHOLE ALLSPICE BERRIES

2 POUNDS (1 KG) FRESH SORREL, WASHED

2 CUPS (480 ML) SUGAR

2 OUNCES (60 ML) JAMAICAN WHITE RUM OR RED WINE

In a large pot, combine the water, rice, ginger, cloves, and allspice. Bring to a boil and add the sorrel. Remove from the heat, cover, and let stand for 24 hours. Strain off the liquid and add the sugar and rum, stirring until the sugar is dissolved. Pour into bottles and refrigerate.

Festival Bread

ALFRE WOODARD AND RODERICK SPENCER

Festival Bread is quite famous and is easy to find in Jamaica at Hellshire Beach in Kingston. It's often served with fried fish or ackee and salt fish, though it's such a daily staple that it can be enjoyed with many different dishes.

Makes 16 pieces

CANOLA OIL, FOR FRYING

1 CUP (240 ML) GROUND YELLOW CORNMEAL

¾ CUP (180 ML) ALL-PURPOSE FLOUR

¼ CUP (60 ML) BROWN SUGAR

½ TEASPOON (2.5 ML) SALT

1 TEASPOON (5 ML) BAKING POWDER

¾–1 CUP (180–240 ML) COLD WATER

In a large deep pot, heat 1" (2.5 cm) of oil to 350°F (180°C).

Meanwhile, in a large bowl, combine the cornmeal, flour, brown sugar, salt, and baking powder. Add ¾ cup (180 ml) water and mix to form dough, adding more water, if necessary. Divide the dough into pieces, ½ tablespoon (7.5 ml) each, and roll into ovals. Slip into the oil and fry for 3 to 5 minutes, or until golden.

GRENADA

A Brief History of Grenada

The island's earliest known inhabitants were the Arawak Indians, who were displaced by the Caribs in about 1400. Although Columbus was the first European to set eyes on Grenada, he doesn't appear to have landed on her shores. The first Europeans to actually settle on the island were the British in 1609, but the Caribs, unhappy about the intrusion, ran them off shortly thereafter. Next came the French, who controlled the island until it was ceded to the British under the Treaty of Paris in 1763. The island went back and forth between the British and the French until it returned to British rule under the Treaty of Versailles in 1783. The island didn't gain its independence until 1974.

Grenada's turbulent history is reflected in the many forts that still command the heights over-looking St. George's Harbor. Several were erected by the French to fight off the British, including Fort George, which was built in 1704.

Anyone who's visited Grenada can certainly understand why nations would fight over it. Just 133 square miles, including its sister islands of Carriacou and Petite Martinique, Grenada boasts pristine beaches surrounded by clear blue seas filled with coral formations that have built up over a millennium or more. The island's hills and valleys are lush with tropical vegetation, and even in the wake of Hurricane Ivan, the beaches are as beautiful as ever.

MORGAN FREEMAN AND MYRNA COLLEY-LEE

SAILING SOUTH TO THE SPICE ISLAND

Myrna Colley-Lee and Morgan Freeman have been married for almost 24 years, and some of their most cherished memories are their many sailing trips from the US and the Virgin Islands down to Grenada. They returned to Grenada in late 2004 to see firsthand the damage inflicted by Hurricane Ivan, and they were deeply saddened to see the wreckage that had once been the homes and businesses of the close friends they had made among the locals over the years.

"We have been back since the hurricane," says Myrna, "but didn't venture up-island, which used to be a favorite thing to do. We would go up into the interior to the rain forest for day trips with friends. There are lots of great little towns and restaurants, which are now, unfortunately, pretty much a mess. So many of the plantations and their crops, such as nutmeg and cinnamon, are gone, literally ripped out of the ground."

But amid the devastation, much renewal is under way. The fishing and seafood industry is back up and running, and this is very good news for Myrna. A lover of everything fish ("I haven't met a fish I didn't like"), she marvels at the local fishermen, who, on occasion, can literally snatch the day's catch out of the crystal-blue water with their hands.

Myrna and Morgan once caught a fish from the boat but didn't know to scale it over the side. As a result, there were fish scales all over everything on the boat for several weeks afterward. So now Myrna buys local fish already scaled to cook on the boat. She also buys spiny lobster from the fishermen who travel around in their skiffs tending their traps. The fishermen either pull up next to anchored boats to sell their live catch or boil their freshly caught lobsters over fires right on the beach and sell them precooked.

When the couple is not dining on deck, two of Myrna's favorite restaurants on Grenada are the Aquarium Restaurant and the True Blue Waterfront Restaurant. A frequented restaurant at the Secret Harbour Resort was completely devastated by the hurricane, but it is now almost rebuilt.

Some of Myrna and Morgan's best times together have been spent sailing from the Virgin Islands down to Trinidad and back up to Grenada, then island-hopping their way back north. "He is always the captain, and I am the first mate," she explains. Their galley is nicely equipped with a three-burner stove, an oven, a freezer, and enough cupboard space to hold canned goods for several weeks of onboard adventures. Myrna calls herself the queen of canned goods, and by mixing six or seven kinds of vegetables, she can create a delicious stew. She can even make gazpacho by combining canned corn, stewed tomatoes, chopped succotash, and a little bit of island pepper sauce.

"At anchor or dockside, I can really prepare anything and everything on the boat," says Myrna. "You can't always find a lot of fresh food, especially familiar vegetables, and salad greens are very hard to find. Some islands have fresh local produce like yams, dasheen, christophene, callaloo, and other melon/squash-type things that I can adapt to several different recipes. I also use lots and lots of bananas and mangoes. On Trinidad and Grenada, they must grow at least a hundred kinds of luscious fruits, all of which are wonderful.

"However, cooking on the boat while we're under way creates more of a challenge than I can handle, because I get seasick. Once we dock or anchor, I'm fine, because we are virtually sitting still. So the morning before we sail, I make some sandwiches and cut up some fruits and veggies and keep them near the companionway so that I don't have to go too far below. Or, if our granddaughter is with us, she'll go down and get cold drinks because she doesn't get seasick.

"We love to go to Grand Anse Beach, and I have spent many memorable evenings cooking out there on the boat, looking at that white silt beach that goes on forever. Grenada is just a beautiful place—not too overdeveloped and very peaceful. You can go into town for many of the modern conveniences and then slip away to a cove or go on a day trip into the rain forest and disappear very quickly. It's been a wonderful retreat for us over the past decade, and I look forward to seeing it revitalized, rebuilt, and restored to its former beauty."

Okra 'n Rice

FROM THE KITCHEN OF MYRNA COLLEY-LEE

"Make sure to sauté the okra first to close up the ends," urges Myrna. *"This cuts down on the slightly slimy texture that gives this vegetable a bad name. This is a very tasty side dish."*

Makes 4 servings

2 CANS (14½ OUNCES [411 G] EACH) STEWED
  TOMATOES

4 TABLESPOONS (60 ML) OLIVE OIL

1 ONION, DICED

2 CLOVES GARLIC, CHOPPED

½ CUP (120 ML) DICED CELERY

½ CUP (120 ML) DICED SALT PORK

2 CUPS (480 ML) SLICED OKRA

¼ CUP (60 ML) CHOPPED FLAT-LEAF PARSLEY

1 TABLESPOON (15 ML) CHOPPED FRESH THYME
  OR 1 TEASPOON (5 ML) DRIED THYME

SALT

FRESHLY GROUND BLACK PEPPER

HOT SAUCE

2 CUPS (480 ML) LONG-GRAIN WHITE RICE

Drain the tomatoes through a sieve into a large bowl. Measure the liquid and add enough water to equal 4 cups (1 L). Set aside.

In a large heavy pot or Dutch oven, heat the oil over medium-high heat. Add the onion, garlic, celery, and salt pork and sauté until lightly colored, about 5 minutes. Add the okra and cook, stirring often, until browned. Stir in the tomatoes and cook until caramelized. Add the parsley and thyme. Add salt, pepper, and hot sauce to taste, then add the rice and tomato liquid/water mixture. Bring to a boil, then reduce the heat to low and simmer, covered, for 1 hour, or until the rice is tender and all the water is absorbed. Taste and season again, if necessary.

NOTE: *Due to the texture of the okra, the vegetable/tomato mixture may stick to the bottom of the pot and burn slightly. If necessary, add a bit more oil, reduce the heat slightly, and stir constantly. After adding the liquid, scrape the bottom of the pan. A little smokiness from the charred vegetable mixture adds flavor to the finished dish.*

Stuffed Red Snapper

FROM THE KITCHEN OF LINDA LEE MILLER

This is one of Myrna's favorite fish dishes. Her sister Linda perfected it and often prepared it for family get-togethers. "Linda couldn't just cook for two or even four people," Myrna explains. "Meals at Linda's usually started with 'let me run into the kitchen and prepare a little something' and ended up a feast. She loved to make Caribbean food—and almost any food, in fact, of the African Diaspora. "We wanted to honor her memory by putting her recipe in the book," says Myrna about her dear sister, who passed in 2003 of lung cancer.

"Linda adapted the recipe from snapper recipes she had tasted, prepared by her husband's family in Louisiana," explains Myrna. "His family was kind of an island blend with Creole blood. They knew a lot about Southern cooking and mixed it all up to create this dish. Linda, of course, added her own kind of flair—and stuffing, because she loved stuffing. I like to serve this with Okra 'n Rice." (See recipe on opposite page.)

Makes 4 servings

6 SLICES FIRM-TEXTURED WHITE BREAD, CRUSTS REMOVED, CUT INTO ½" (1.25 CM) CUBES

10 TABLESPOONS (150 ML) UNSALTED BUTTER

¼ CUP (60 ML) CHOPPED CELERY

¼ CUP(60 ML) CHOPPED ONION

¼ CUP (60 ML) CHOPPED SCALLIONS (WHITE PARTS AND ½" [1.25 CM] OF GREEN PARTS)

2 CLOVES GARLIC, CHOPPED

½ CUP (120 ML) CHOPPED MEDIUM SHRIMP

½ CUP (120 ML) CHOPPED PICKED-OVER LUMP CRABMEAT

4 DROPS HOT SAUCE

PINCH OF DRY MUSTARD

1 TEASPOON (5 ML) SALT + MORE FOR SEASONING

½ TEASPOON (2.5 ML) FRESHLY GROUND BLACK PEPPER + MORE FOR SEASONING

1 LARGE RED SNAPPER (ABOUT 4 POUNDS [1.8 KG]), CLEANED, OR 4 FILLETS (12 OUNCES [340 G] EACH)

5 OR 6 SPRIGS FRESH THYME, MARJORAM, OR OREGANO

¼ CUP (60 ML) DRY WHITE WINE

¼ CUP (60 ML) WATER

1 BAY LEAF

Spread the bread cubes on a baking sheet or large pan and let stand to dry overnight, stirring occasionally so they dry evenly. (Alternatively, dry the bread in a 275°F [135°C] oven until slightly browned, stirring frequently so it dries evenly and doesn't burn.) Transfer to a food processor and process into crumbs. Set aside.

(CONTINUED)

Preheat the oven to 350°F (180°C). Grease a baking dish or roasting pan, large enough to hold the fish, with butter or vegetable oil.

In a large skillet, melt 4 tablespoons (60 ml) of the butter over medium-high heat. Add the celery, onion, scallions, and garlic and sauté for 1 to 2 minutes, or until soft. Add the shrimp and cook, stirring, for about 30 seconds. Transfer to a large bowl and add the crabmeat, hot sauce, mustard, the 1 teaspoon (5 ml) salt, and the ½ teaspoon (2.5 ml) pepper. Stir in the bread crumbs.

In a separate pan, melt the remaining 6 tablespoons (90 ml) butter. Pour 4 tablespoons (60 ml) of the melted butter over the bread crumb mixture and toss well, making sure it is evenly moistened.

Rinse the fish and dry well. If preparing a whole fish, brush the inside with a small amount of the remaining 2 tablespoons (30 ml) melted butter and season to taste with salt and pepper. Spoon the stuffing into the fish, filling it completely. Make 3 gashes on each side of the fish, brush with the remaining melted butter, season with salt and pepper, and transfer to the prepared baking dish. Place the fresh herbs over the gashes. If preparing fillets, divide the stuffing into 4 portions and arrange in a large baking dish. Lay a fillet, skin-side up, over each portion.

In a small bowl, combine the wine and water and pour the liquid around the fish. Add the bay leaf and bake, basting frequently, for 50 to 60 minutes if you're preparing one large fish, or 20 to 25 minutes if you're preparing fillets, until the flesh is firm to the touch. Strain the pan drippings and serve as a sauce.

Jessica's Tropical Pancakes with Ginger Syrup

FROM THE KITCHEN OF JESSICA FASMAN

Jessica Fasman is one of Myrna's oldest and dearest friends. A great home cook and amateur caterer, Jessica created this tropical pancakes recipe especially for the book. A costume designer by profession, she also served as the test kitchen chef for all of Myrna's recipes. "I love to cook," she says "especially baking, and some of my most memorable meals have been shared with Morgan and Myrna. While I was helping Myrna with these recipes, I started thinking about the flavorful fruits in the Caribbean. I developed this recipe and thought of how wonderful it would be to eat these pancakes as part of a leisurely brunch overlooking the Caribbean Sea on a terrace, feeling the breeze from the ocean and feeling totally content." Instead of serving these with ginger syrup, you can serve them with whipped cream or yogurt.

Makes 4 servings

PANCAKES

1 CUP (240 ML) SIFTED CAKE FLOUR

1 TEASPOON (5 ML) SUGAR

½ TEASPOON (2.5 ML) SALT

¾ TEASPOON (3.7 ML) BAKING POWDER

½ TEASPOON (2.5 ML) BAKING SODA

1 EGG

1 CUP (240 ML) BUTTERMILK

2 TABLESPOONS (30 ML) UNSALTED BUTTER, MELTED + MORE FOR COOKING

GRATED ZEST OF 1 LEMON

GINGER SYRUP

1 VANILLA BEAN POD, SPLIT LENGTHWISE

½ CUP (120 ML) WATER

1 CUP (240 ML) SUGAR

1" (2.5 CM) PIECE FRESH GINGER, PEELED AND CHOPPED

PEEL FROM ½ LEMON, CUT INTO PIECES

FRUIT

1 TABLESPOON (15 ML) UNSALTED BUTTER

¼ LARGE RIPE PINEAPPLE, PEELED, CORED, SLICED, AND CUT INTO 1" (2.5 CM) WEDGES

1 MANGO, PEELED, PITTED, AND CUBED

1 MEDIUM PAPAYA, PEELED, SEEDED, AND CUBED

1 LARGE BANANA, SLICED THICK

1 RECIPE GINGER SYRUP

½ TEASPOON (2.5 ML) CINNAMON

GARNISH

¼ CUP (60 ML) FRESH RASPBERRIES

2–3 TABLESPOONS (30–45 ML) COARSELY GRATED TOASTED COCONUT

CONFECTIONERS' SUGAR AND/OR CINNAMON

TO MAKE THE PANCAKES: Resift the flour with the sugar, salt, baking powder, and baking soda into a large bowl. Beat the egg until light and slightly thickened. Mix in the buttermilk and the 2 tablespoons (30 ml) melted butter. Pour the liquid ingredients over the dry ingredients, add the lemon zest, and stir until just combined. (Do not overmix.) The batter can be refrigerated tightly covered, overnight.

TO MAKE THE GINGER SYRUP: Scrape the seeds out of the vanilla bean pod and set both aside.

In a small nonreactive saucepan (preferably nonstick), combine the water and sugar and place over medium heat. Swirl the mixture once or twice, but do not stir it. When the sugar has melted, add the ginger, vanilla bean and seeds, and lemon peel. Continue cooking until the mixture comes to a boil. Lower the heat and simmer, swirling occasionally, until slightly thickened and syrupy. (It will thicken more as it cools.) Remove from the heat, cool, and strain through a fine sieve. If not using immediately, cover and refrigerate.

TO MAKE THE FRUIT: Melt the butter in a large heavy skillet over medium heat. Add the pineapple and sauté for 2 minutes, then add the mango, papaya, and banana and cook, stirring carefully. Once the fruit has begun to brown slightly, add about half the Ginger Syrup and all of the cinnamon; continue cooking and stirring until the fruit mixture is heated through and very fragrant, adding more Ginger Syrup, if necessary. Reserve the rest of the Ginger Syrup.

TO COOK THE PANCAKES AND ASSEMBLE: Preheat the oven to 200°F (93°C). Preheat a griddle over medium heat until drops of cold water dance across the surface. Lightly brush the griddle with the additional melted butter and pour a scant ¼ cup (60 ml) of batter for each pancake. Cook until bubbles appear on the upper surface of the pancakes and the edges look slightly brown, then turn carefully and cook on the second side, until lightly browned. Stack the finished pancakes, separated by a linen tea towel or waxed paper, and keep them warm in the oven.

When all the pancakes are cooked, brush them with a bit of melted butter and place in stacks of 3 on serving plates. Spoon the fruit over the pancakes and top with a few raspberries and some toasted coconut. Sprinkle some confectioners' sugar and/or cinnamon from a sieve around the plate for decoration. Serve with the reserved Ginger Syrup.

NOTE: *For perfectly round pancakes, place well-buttered rings on the griddle and spoon the batter into them. Make sure not to overfill the rings, as the batter will rise as it cooks. Run the point of a knife around the edges of the pancakes, if necessary, to release them from the rings. Remove the rings and then turn the pancakes carefully.*

Baked Banana Pudding

FROM THE KITCHENS OF MYRNA COLLEY-LEE AND JESSICA FASMAN

Makes 8 servings

2 VERY RIPE BANANAS

2 TABLESPOONS (30 ML) FRESH LIME JUICE

⅓ CUP (80 ML) UNSALTED BUTTER, AT ROOM TEMPERATURE

1 CUP (240 ML) FIRMLY PACKED LIGHT BROWN SUGAR

4 EGGS, AT ROOM TEMPERATURE

2 TEASPOONS (10 ML) VANILLA EXTRACT

¼ TEASPOON (1.2 ML) SALT

½ TEASPOON (2.5 ML) FRESHLY GROUND NUTMEG

⅓ CUP (80 ML) ALL-PURPOSE FLOUR

⅓ CUP (80 ML) UNSWEETENED COCONUT MILK OR HEAVY CREAM

1 TABLESPOON (15 ML) COCONUT RUM

HEAVY CREAM

½ CUP (120 ML) CHOPPED PECANS OR WALNUTS, TOASTED AND COOLED

Preheat the oven to 350°F (180°C). Butter a 13" x 9" (32.5 x 23 cm) baking pan and set aside.

Peel and mash the bananas in a small bowl and stir in the lime juice.

In a medium bowl and using an electric mixer, cream together the butter and sugar until light and fluffy. Add the eggs one at a time, beating well after each addition, then add the vanilla extract. Scrape down the sides of the bowl to make sure the ingredients are completely blended.

In another medium bowl, whisk the salt and nutmeg into the flour. Add the flour to the butter/sugar mixture in 2 batches, alternating with the banana/lime juice mixture. Beat well.

In a small bowl, combine the coconut milk or cream and the rum and stir into the banana mixture.

Pour the batter into the prepared pan and bake in the center of the oven for 45 minutes to 1 hour, until set. Serve with the cream and toasted nuts.

VARIATION: For Cherry Coconut Banana Pudding, replace the vanilla extract with ¼ teaspoon (1.2 ml) almond extract. Pour boiling water over ¾ cup (180 ml) dried cherries and soak for ½ hour, then drain well. Stir the cherries into the batter after adding the coconut milk and rum. Bake the pudding for ½ hour, then sprinkle with a thick layer of shredded, sweetened coconut, and bake an additional 15 to 20 minutes, until the coconut is golden. Decorate the finished pudding with fresh cherries.

Trotters Broth

TROTTERS RESTAURANT, OWNER GARFIELD PATTERSON

Garfield Patterson is a Grenadian businessman who owns a boutique on the Carenage, which is a frequent stop for tourists from cruise ships and stay-over passengers. He sells packaged spices, scented soaps, and locally made clothing. Garfield lost his house during Ivan. He and his 70-year-old mother sought refuge in the bottom cupboard of their kitchen sink after their roof blew off during the storm.

"Trotters" or "Pig Souse" is a very popular local dish. Made by families for special occasions, it is perfect for a picnic at the beach. The spices included in the sauce and the "waters" of the dish make people yearn for more.

Makes 4 to 6 servings

3 POUNDS (1.4 KG) PIG'S FEET, WELL CLEANED, OR 1 POUND (454 G) BONELESS PORK LOIN

2 LARGE ONIONS, DICED

2 TABLESPOONS (30 ML) MINCED GARLIC

2 SEASONING PEPPERS (GREEN AND YELLOW), SEEDED AND CHOPPED (SEE RESOURCES, PAGE 246)

1 SPRIG FRESH THYME

SALT

JUICE OF 4 LIMES

2 LARGE CUCUMBERS, THINLY SLICED

1 RIB CELERY, THINLY SLICED

HOT PEPPER SAUCE

In a pressure cooker, combine the pig's feet or pork and half the onions, garlic, and seasoning peppers. Add the thyme and season to taste with the salt. Cook according to the manufacturer's directions until the pig's feet or pork is tender, 30 to 35 minutes for pig's feet or 15 minutes for pork loin. Rinse the pig's feet or pork in cold water and, when cool enough to handle, slice into bite-size pieces.

In a large bowl, combine the lime juice and enough water to equal 3 cups (720 ml). Add the remaining onions, garlic, and seasoning peppers, as well as the cucumbers and celery. Season to taste with hot pepper sauce and additional salt, if desired. Pour the sauce over the pork and refrigerate for 3 to 4 hours before serving.

Tuna with Orange, Ginger, and Lemongrass Sauce

BROWN SUGAR, PROPRIETOR/EXECUTIVE CHEF PATRICK DAVID

Brown Sugar Restaurant, formerly South Winds Restaurant, has been a Grenada staple since 1990. Patrick David, the restaurant's owner, loves creating innovative cuisine and new dishes using island staples like dasheen. The restaurant is consistently recommended by travel agents and those in the know when it comes to great food on Grenada, and Myrna and Morgan have spent many a lazy evening chatting with friends while a never-ending parade of tasty food made its way to their table.

Makes 8 servings

2 TABLESPOONS (30 ML) BUTTER OR MARGARINE

2 TABLESPOONS (30 ML) OLIVE OIL + ADDITIONAL FOR GRILLING

2 ONIONS, FINELY CHOPPED

4 TABLESPOONS (60 ML) PEELED AND MINCED FRESH GINGER

4 TABLESPOONS (60 ML) MINCED FRESH LEMONGRASS

2 TABLESPOONS (30 ML) MINCED GARLIC

2 TABLESPOONS (30 ML) FLOUR

1 CUP (240 ML) FRESH ORANGE JUICE

1 CHICKEN BOUILLON CUBE AND 1 VEGETABLE BOUILLON CUBE DISSOLVED INTO 2 CUPS (480 ML) WATER

3 TABLESPOONS (45 ML) SOY SAUCE

1 TEASPOON (5 ML) HOT PEPPER SAUCE

SALT

FRESHLY GROUND BLACK PEPPER

8 (6–7 OUNCES [170–198 G] EACH) TUNA STEAKS

FRESH LIME JUICE

GREEN SEASONING (SEE RESOURCES, PAGE 245)

In a saucepan, heat the butter or margarine and the 2 tablespoons (30 ml) oil. Add the onions, ginger, lemongrass, and garlic and sauté for 2 minutes. Sprinkle the flour over the mixture and stir until combined, about 1 minute, but do not allow the flour to brown. Gradually stir in the orange juice, bouillon, and soy sauce. When well blended, add the pepper sauce and salt and pepper to taste. Continue to simmer for 10 minutes, or until thickened.

Season the tuna steaks to taste with the lime juice, green seasoning, salt, and pepper. Brush them with oil and sear on a hot griddle, until opaque in the center, about 3 minutes per side. Bring the sauce back to a simmer. Transfer the fish to 8 dinner plates and serve with sauce drizzled over each portion.

Island Crab, Mango, Ground Nuts, and Cucumber Salad, with Mango Vinaigrette

BROWN SUGAR, EXECUTIVE CHEF PATRICK DAVID

Makes 4 servings

MANGO VINAIGRETTE

2 TABLESPOONS (30 ML) OLIVE OIL

1 LARGE RIPE MANGO, PEELED, PITTED, AND DICED

SALT

FRESHLY GROUND WHITE PEPPER

¼ CUP (60 ML) WATER

1 TEASPOON (5 ML) FRESHLY SQUEEZED LEMON JUICE

1½ TABLESPOONS (22.5 ML) WHITE VINEGAR

SALAD

1 POUND (454 G) LUMP CRABMEAT

3 TABLESPOONS (45 ML) LIME JUICE

6 TABLESPOONS (90 ML) EXTRA-VIRGIN OLIVE OIL

2 TABLESPOONS (30 ML) HOT PEPPER SAUCE

2 TABLESPOONS (30 ML) FINELY CHOPPED CILANTRO

3 TEASPOONS (15 ML) DRIED SPEARMINT

SALT

FRESHLY GROUND WHITE PEPPER

2 MEDIUM MANGOES, PEELED, PITTED, AND CUT INTO ½" (1.25 CM) PIECES

2 CUCUMBERS, PEELED, SEEDED, AND CUT INTO ½" (1.25 CM) PIECES

4 TABLESPOONS (60 ML) UNSALTED PEANUTS, TOASTED AND COARSELY CHOPPED

WHOLE CILANTRO, FOR GARNISH

WHOLE MINT LEAVES, FOR GARNISH

TO MAKE THE VINAIGRETTE: In a small pan, heat the oil over medium heat. Add the mango, season to taste with salt and pepper, and cook, stirring, for about 3 minutes, until the fruit is very tender. Add the ¼ cup (60 ml) water, bring to a boil, and remove the pan from the heat. Stir in the lemon juice and vinegar and transfer the mixture to a blender. Puree until smooth. Cool and chill until needed.

TO MAKE THE SALAD: Combine the crabmeat with 2 tablespoons (30 ml) of the lime juice, half of the oil, half of the pepper sauce, and two-thirds of the chopped cilantro and mint. Season to taste with salt and pepper. Toss lightly with a fork. Divide the salad among 4 dinner plates.

In a separate bowl, combine the mangoes and cucumbers. Add the remaining lime juice, oil, pepper sauce, cilantro, and mint. Season to taste with salt and pepper. Scatter the mixture over each serving and sprinkle with the peanuts. Top with the cilantro and mint, and surround with the Mango Vinaigrette.

The Red Crab Crab Backs

THE RED CRAB, GRENADA, CHEF/OWNER GEORGE MULLER

The Red Crab is the place for West Indian cuisine on the island, and the restaurant's chef is known for having an expert hand when it comes to spices. Located in L'anse aux Epines, near quaint island cottages and some of the island's favorite lodging for visitors, the restaurant is always packed on the weekends. This dish, the restaurant's premiere signature, is one reason. For an exciting appetizer presentation, ask your fishmonger for large cleaned shells.

Makes 4 servings

½ POUND (227 G) LUMP CRABMEAT

4 TABLESPOONS (60 ML) UNSALTED BUTTER

1 ONION, CHOPPED

1 TOMATO, DICED

2 CLOVES GARLIC, MINCED

3 FRESH CHIVES, CHOPPED

1 TABLESPOON (15 ML) WORCESTERSHIRE SAUCE

SALT

FRESHLY GROUND BLACK PEPPER

1 DOZEN LARGE CLEAN CRAB SHELLS (OPTIONAL)

¼ CUP (60 ML) DRIED BREAD CRUMBS

HOT PEPPER SAUCE (OPTIONAL)

Pick over crabmeat to remove any pieces of shell.

Preheat the oven to 350°F (180°C). Coat 4 (½-cup [120-ml]) ramekins with cooking spray and set aside.

In a large skillet, heat 2 tablespoons (30 ml) of the butter. Add the onion, tomato, garlic, and chives and sauté until lightly browned, about 5 minutes. Add the crabmeat and Worcestershire sauce, season with salt and pepper, and cook, stirring, for 4 to 5 minutes, until the crab is cooked through. Remove from the heat and set aside to cool for 3 minutes.

Divide the crabmeat mixture among the prepared ramekins. If using cleaned crab shells, divide crabmeat mixture among them. Sprinkle with the bread crumbs and dot with the remaining 2 tablespoons (30 ml) butter. Put the ramekins or filled shells on a baking sheet and brown in the oven for 5 minutes. Serve with a dash of hot sauce, if desired.

Spicy Crab Cakes
with Sweet Cucumber Vinaigrette

THE BEACH HOUSE, GENERAL MANAGER/EXECUTIVE CHEF STANLEY MINORS

On a shaded terrace overlooking the white sandy beaches that lure couples to tie the knot, the Beach House is one of the most romantic restaurants on Grenada. Homemade dishes that feature fish and seafood are the favorites here.

Makes 6 servings

VINAIGRETTE

¼ CUP (60 ML) DISTILLED WHITE VINEGAR

2½ TABLESPOONS (32.5 ML) SUGAR

1 TABLESPOON (15 ML) FRESH LIME JUICE

1 TABLESPOON (15 ML) WATER

1 TEASPOON (5 ML) MINCED RED CHILI PEPPER

½ TEASPOON (2.5 ML) MINCED GARLIC

1½ TEASPOONS (7.5 ML) POPPY SEEDS

1½ TEASPOONS (7.5 ML) WHITE SESAME SEEDS, TOASTED

3 TABLESPOONS (45 ML) SEEDED AND GRATED CUCUMBER

CRAB CAKES

1 POUND (454 G) LUMP CRABMEAT

1 LARGE ONION, FINELY CHOPPED

1 TABLESPOON (15 ML) MINCED GARLIC

1 RIB CELERY, DICED

3 TABLESPOONS (45 ML) FRESH CHIVES, CHOPPED

6 SEASONING PEPPERS, DICED (SEE RESOURCES, PAGE 246)

½ TEASPOON (2.5 ML) SALT

½ TEASPOON (2.5 ML) FRESHLY GROUND BLACK PEPPER

2 TEASPOONS (10 ML) HOT SAUCE

1 TEASPOON (5 ML) RED PEPPER FLAKES

2 TEASPOONS (10 ML) CHOPPED FRESH THYME

2 TEASPOONS (10 ML) LIME JUICE

2 TABLESPOONS (30 ML) OLIVE OIL

1 CUP (240 ML) GROUND WHEAT CRACKERS

2 LARGE EGGS, BEATEN

VEGETABLE OIL, FOR FRYING

TO MAKE THE VINAIGRETTE: In a large bowl, combine the vinegar, sugar, lime juice, water, chili pepper, garlic, poppy seeds, sesame seeds, and cucumber. Cover and refrigerate until ready to use.

TO MAKE THE CRAB CAKES: In a large bowl, combine the crabmeat, onion, garlic, celery, chives, seasoning peppers, salt, pepper, hot sauce, red pepper flakes, thyme, lime juice, oil, and cracker crumbs. Toss gently to combine. Add the eggs and mix well. Form the crab mixture into 2" (5 cm) patties.

In a large skillet, heat 1" (2.5 cm) of oil to 360°F (182°C) and fry the crab cakes on both sides until cooked through and golden brown, about 1 minute total. Serve warm with vinaigrette on the side.

Sunburst Mahi Mahi

DE BIG FISH, CHEF BRADLEY TAYLOR

At True Blue's Spice Island Marina, De Big Fish is the popular spot for the locals and boating folks. Drinks and good music flow from its spacious deck-styled dining floor and into the lagoon as guests dine on great food that ranges from the casual to the complex. Bradley Taylor, the restaurant's innovative Canadian-Grenadian chef/owner, often adds new and exciting dishes. This mahi mahi is a popular take on a standard island fish.

Makes 2 servings

2 FILLETS (6 OUNCES [170 G] EACH) MAHI MAHI
SALT
FRESHLY GROUND BLACK PEPPER
2 TABLESPOONS (30 ML) OLIVE OIL
¼ CUP (60 ML) BREAD CRUMBS
¼ CUP (60 ML) FINELY GRATED COCONUT

¼ CUP (60 ML) CASSAVA FLOUR OR WHOLE WHEAT FLOUR
1 CUP (240 ML) MASHED SWEET POTATO
DASHEEN CHIPS (SEE NOTE)
MANGO SALSA (RECIPE FOLLOWS)

Preheat the oven to 350°F (180°C).

Season the fish with salt and pepper and rub with a light coat of oil, reserving the rest.

In a bowl, combine the bread crumbs, coconut, and flour and roll the fish in the mixture, making sure it is well coated. Transfer the coated fish to a plate and refrigerate for a few minutes.

In a large, ovenproof nonstick skillet, heat the remaining oil and fry the fish on 1 side for 1 minute. Slip the skillet into the oven and bake for 8 to 10 minutes, until the fish is opaque.

Heat the sweet potato and center a portion on each dinner plate. Place fillet on top and stick the dasheen chips into the sweet potato, creating a flower petal effect. Cover the fish generously with the salsa.

(CONTINUED)

MANGO SALSA

1 MANGO, PEELED, PITTED, AND DICED

¼ CUP (60 ML) DICED RED ONION

2 SEASONING PEPPERS, SEEDED AND DICED (SEE
   RESOURCES, PAGE 246)

2 GREEN CHILE PEPPERS, CHOPPED (SEE NOTE)

1 TABLESPOON (15 ML) HONEY

1 TABLESPOON (15 ML) LIME JUICE

2 PINCHES OF CHILI POWDER

2 PINCHES OF GRATED LIME ZEST

In a large bowl, combine the mango, onion, seasoning peppers, chile peppers, honey, lime juice, chili powder, and lime zest. Toss to combine. Let stand for about 30 minutes before serving.

NOTE: *To make dasheen (also known as taro) chips, peel and cut the dasheen into large pieces. Boil for a few minutes in salted water. Drain and refrigerate for a few hours. Cut into very thin slices, pat dry, and fry until lightly browned in oil that has been heated to 360°F (182°C). Season to taste with salt. Store in an airtight container for up to 2 days.*

Wear plastic gloves when handling chile peppers, and wash your hands thoroughly with soap and water before touching sensitive parts of your body, especially your face. To reduce the heat in the finished dish, use only the sides of the pepper (discard seeds and core).

Ginger Beer

DE BIG FISH, CHEF BRADLEY TAYLOR

In the Caribbean island strand, ginger is favored for its ability to calm an upset stomach or tame a cold, but the pungent root enhances any dish it accompanies. This beer recipe, developed by Chef Bradley, is a great complement to crab cakes and salty dishes.

Makes 16 (1 cup [240 ml]) servings

1 POUND (454 G) FRESH GINGER, PEELED

2¾ CUPS (660 ML) LUKEWARM WATER (95°–100°F [35°–38°C])

⅛ TEASPOON (0.6 ML) ACTIVE DRY YEAST

2¼ CUPS (540 ML) SUGAR

12 CUPS (2.8 L) HOT WATER (120°–125°F [48°–52°C])

Grate the ginger into a mixing bowl, using the finer side of the grater (or use a food processor with grater attachment). Add 2 cups (480 ml) of the lukewarm water and stir the mixture for 1 to 2 minutes, then allow it to settle for 5 minutes. Stir again, then strain through a fine sieve, catching all the liquid in a bowl. Collect the pulp in your hands or cheesecloth and squeeze thoroughly to extract all the remaining liquid. (The better the squeeze, the stronger the flavor.) Stir and measure out 2 cups (480 ml) of the liquid.

In a small bowl, combine the yeast with the remaining ¾ cup (180 ml) lukewarm water and stir just enough to moisten. Set aside for 10 minutes, uncovered.

In a large, nonreactive bowl or pot, combine the sugar and hot water. Stir until the sugar is completely dissolved and the water appears clear. Stir in the reserved ginger extract. Add the yeast mixture and combine thoroughly.

Using a funnel, transfer the liquid to soda bottles, leaving at least 1" (2.5 cm) at the top of each bottle. Cap the bottles tightly and stand them upright in a warm place for 5 to 6 days, until the beer is effervescent. Refrigerate before serving.

Grenada's Agriculture
and the Road to Recovery

Grenada's natural landscape has begun to regenerate since Hurricane Ivan, but the same is unfortunately not yet true of the island's agriculture. One of the hardest hit economies has been the farming and spice trade, and it will take many, many years for the farms and plantations to once again be at full production. Once the debris has been cleared, short crops—such as bananas, seasoning peppers, and most other vegetables—will be planted, and production will begin.

Since the 16th century, Grenada has been known for its lucrative spice crops. Before Ivan, Grenada grew more spices per square mile than any other place on Earth. Its signature nutmeg trees first arrived in 1843 and were planted at the Penang Estate in St. Andrew Parish. In 2002, nutmeg, along with allspice (Jamaican pepper), bay leaves, cocoa, cloves, cinnamon, ginger, turmeric, and vanilla, accounted for 16 percent of the island's annual export revenues. What was once the island's second-biggest moneymaker after tourism has been largely destroyed.

THE GRENADIAN SPICE TRADE IS SPRINGING BACK

Vivian Purcell is the owner of Pleasant Estate, the largest producer of nutmeg, cloves, and cocoa on the island. In Hurricane Ivan and its aftermath, he lost the house that had been in his family for more than 40 years and also more than 70 percent of his nutmeg trees, 80 percent of his clove crop,

and many of his cinnamon and cocoa plants. Some of his trees had been growing for more than 100 years, but because nutmeg and clove trees have such shallow roots, they were literally ripped from the ground and tossed around as if they were saplings.

"Fortunately," says Mr. Purcell, "the soil was not damaged and is still very rich. We started planting nutmeg trees just weeks after Ivan, but unfortunately these trees are very slow growing and take a long time to start bearing fruit. It really takes 15 years for them to reach full growth and produce a mature crop.

"Ivan has been incredibly damaging to Grenada and to me personally," he goes on. "Before the hurricane, the plantation would sell $3,000 to $4,000 worth of nutmeg a week, but right now we can't even sell $300 worth a week. After picking up the nutmeg from the ground, we sell it to the Nutmeg Board for processing, so we don't have any inventory, and 3 months after Ivan, we had run out of nutmeg."

Mace, a byproduct of nutmeg that's frequently more valuable than the nutmeg itself (it's used in cosmetics and as a preservative in many foods) is also scarce.

But Mr. Purcell and all of Grenada still pride themselves on being called the Spice Island, and replanting is well under way. The Nutmeg Processing Station in Gouyave continues to offer tours and to sell the spice at pre-Ivan prices, and the local markets are still featuring—although not in as much abundance— the nuts, leaves, and pods that give this tiny island its nickname.

Luckily the cocoa trees, which have much deeper roots, were not so badly damaged, so cocoa has become one of the plantation's biggest crops. "It's not a lot, but every bit helps," says Mr. Purcell, who believes that because Grenada has the richest and best-tasting cocoa in the world, other countries buy it to blend with their own.

Mr. Purcell prides himself on his dark and fragrant hot chocolate recipe, which he was kind enough to share.

Fresh raw nutmeg at a local market

The Spices of Grenada

NUTMEG: The nutmeg fruit is round and yellow and grows on trees that can reach 60 feet tall. The fruit is never harvested until it falls to the ground, at which time it is gathered immediately, the red mace is stripped from the shell, and the two substances are dried separately. An extremely versatile spice, nutmeg is added to everything from rum punch and eggnog to sweet potato and pumpkin recipes, ice cream, and other desserts. It is frequently paired with cinnamon and cloves.

ALLSPICE (JAMAICAN PEPPER): Allspice is the dried berry of the *Pimenta dioica* tree, which is native to the Caribbean. It tastes a bit like a combination of cinnamon, clove, and nutmeg (thus the name). The green fruit, about the size of a pea, changes to dark brown when picked and dried in the sun. Allspice is used to flavor many foods, including gravies and sauces, puddings, cakes and sweet breads, preserves, relishes, and even curry powders.

BAY LEAF: The bay leaf comes from an evergreen tree of the laurel family. It is used to enhance meat and poultry dishes, pickles, soups, and particularly tomato dishes, including pasta sauces and tomato soup.

CINNAMON: Cinnamon is made from the dried bark of another type of evergreen also related to the laurel family. Sold either in sticks or ground, the spice has a sweet, delicate aroma that enhances the flavor of cakes, breads, and pies and makes a delicious topping for broiled or stewed fruits.

CLOVE: A clove is a dried, unopened flower bud of a tree that can grow to a height of 40 feet. Used whole (as for decorating hams) or ground, the spice flavors meat dishes, gravies, cakes, puddings, pies, and even fruit-based beverages such as apple juice and cider.

GINGER: Ginger comes from the root of a plant with a leafy, reedlike stem. In its fresh state, it is used most frequently in Asian cooking. Dried and ground, it is used as a flavoring in cakes, breads, pies, and drinks, such as ginger beer.

TURMERIC: Turmeric resembles gingerroot, except that it is orange-yellow in color. It is a key ingredient in curry powder and also gives mustard its deep yellow color.

VANILLA: Vanilla plants bear long, brown bean pods from which the seeds can be scraped to use as flavoring. The essence is also extracted and sold in liquid form. Both the seeds and the extract are used in sweet dishes, including ice cream and cakes. Vanilla is also used to make perfume, and it is brewed locally and taken to help relieve ailments such as stomachaches, colds, and fever.

Hot Chocolate

FROM THE KITCHEN OF VIVIAN PURCELL

Makes 4 servings

3 CUPS (720 ML) WATER

1 CINNAMON STICK + MORE IF DESIRED

2–3 FRESH OR DRIED BAY LEAVES

1½ OUNCES (42 G) UNSWEETENED CHOCOLATE

¾ CUP (180 ML) EVAPORATED MILK OR CREAM

SUGAR OR CONDENSED MILK

In a saucepan, bring the water to a boil with the cinnamon stick and bay leaves. Add the chocolate and return to a boil. Reduce the heat and simmer until the chocolate melts. Add the milk or cream and return to a boil, stirring occasionally. Remove and discard the bay leaves. Sweeten to taste with the sugar or condensed milk and serve with additional cinnamon sticks, if desired.

RHODES RESTAURANT

Calabash Hotel, Grenada

Gary Rhodes, Owner; Kevin Darbyshire, Executive Chef

When restaurateur Gary Rhodes decided to open his first restaurant outside the United Kingdom, the location he chose was the sprawling Calabash Hotel in Grenada. Executive Chef Kevin Darbyshire, who had been a member of the Rhodes organization in England before taking the helm at the Rhodes Restaurant in Grenada, happened to be on vacation and sitting in a local English pub when he received news of the hurricane.

"My first reaction was that I should have been on the island," he said, "because Grenada was now my home, but my two associates who had stayed told me it was a place I definitely didn't want to be. Galvanized steel was flying off roofs, there were cracks in the pantries, and debris was everywhere. We were lucky it happened in daylight so that most people could get out of harm's way, but most of the island was without electricity, and some parts were without drinking water for weeks.

"Ivan absolutely devastated the food industry here. Every vegetable and fruit—from bananas and mangoes to breadfruit—had to start growing again the day after the storm. Most of the restaurants had to turn to importers to bring in many food items, but even that was difficult because many of them were closed for 6 months, so the orders were very small. When St. George's University reopened in late January, there was a need for many more supplies, and the importing started to open up again."

It took a year and a half, but the Rhodes Restaurant is now fully operational, and guests are once again enjoying Chef Kevin's remarkable cuisine.

Seared Tuna with Cucumber Pickle and Caribbean Coleslaw

RHODES RESTAURANT, CHEF KEVIN DARBYSHIRE

One of the restaurant's most popular appetizers is this Seared Tuna with Cucumber Pickle and Caribbean Coleslaw. "We keep it simple," says Chef Kevin, "and stick with the freshest ingredients possible. This tuna appetizer is a perfect example. The fresher and more colorful the fish, the better the dish will look and taste."

Makes 4 servings

1 TABLESPOON (15 ML) VEGETABLE OIL

1 POUND (454 G) TUNA LOIN, CUT INTO 8 EQUAL PIECES

SEA SALT, CRUSHED

FRESHLY GROUND BLACK PEPPER

1 RECIPE CUCUMBER PICKLE (RECIPE FOLLOWS)

1 RECIPE CARIBBEAN COLESLAW (RECIPE FOLLOWS)

Heat the vegetable oil in a large skillet over high heat. Lightly dust the tuna with salt and pepper and pansear it until crisp on the outside and still moist and pink inside, 1 to 2 minutes. Serve with Cucumber Pickle and Caribbean Coleslaw.

CUCUMBER PICKLE

4 CUCUMBERS, PEELED AND SEEDED

1½ TEASPOONS (7.5 ML) SALT

⅔ CUP (160 ML) PEANUT OIL

1 TEASPOON (5 ML) CHILI OIL

1 LARGE CLOVE GARLIC, CRUSHED

1 FRESH RED CHILE PEPPER, FINELY CHOPPED (SEE NOTE)

2 TABLESPOONS (30 ML) SOY SAUCE

3 TABLESPOONS (45 ML) SUPERFINE GRANULATED SUGAR

2 TABLESPOONS (30 ML) WHITE WINE VINEGAR

½ BUNCH SCALLIONS, WHITE AND GREEN PARTS, THINLY SLICED

Grate the cucumbers on a box-type cheese grater. Place them in a small bowl. Mix in the salt and place the salted cucumbers into a colander to drain for 20 minutes. (This will take out any excess water.)

In a saucepan, warm the peanut oil and chili oil with the garlic and pepper for a few minutes. Add the soy sauce, sugar, and vinegar and bring to a simmer.

Gently pat the cucumbers dry with paper towels. Place them into a small bowl and add the scallions. Add the cucumber mixture to the simmering oil and raise the heat, stirring for 30 seconds. Remove from the heat and tip the pickled cucumbers onto a deep tray or into a large cold saucepan to cool as quickly as possible. Store in an airtight jar.

NOTE: *Wear plastic gloves when handling chile peppers, and wash your hands thoroughly with soap and water before touching sensitive parts of your body, especially your face. To reduce the heat in the finished dish, use only the sides of the pepper (discard seeds and core).*

CARIBBEAN COLESLAW

2 MEDIUM CARROTS, PEELED AND CUT INTO THIN STRIPS

½ CHRISTOPHENE (ALSO KNOWN AS CHAYOTE) OR JICAMA, CUT INTO THIN STRIPS

½ SMALL WHITE ONION, CUT INTO THIN STRIPS

½ POUND (227 G) CABBAGE, CUT INTO THIN STRIPS

SALT

FRESHLY GROUND BLACK PEPPER

4 TABLESPOONS (60 ML) MAYONNAISE

3 TABLESPOONS (45 ML) CHOPPED FRESH CILANTRO OR PARSLEY, FOR GARNISH

PINCH OF SUGAR (OPTIONAL)

In a large bowl, combine the carrots, christophene or jicama, onion, and cabbage. Toss together and season to taste with the salt and pepper. Stir in the mayonnaise. Garnish with the cilantro or parsley and a sprinkling of sugar, if desired. Chill before serving. (This can be made ahead and refrigerated for up to 3 days.)

Hurricane Ivan

"Over the years, we have experienced heavy thunderstorms, but there has been only one hurricane in the known history of the island—Janet—that occurred in September 1955. We do not expect a repeat visit for another five hundred years or so."

—*GRENADA, ISLE OF SPICE*, BY NORMA SINCLAIR (MACMILLAN CARIBBEAN, 2002)

Citizens from the idyllic island of Grenada went into the 2004 hurricane season with the same attitude they've had for almost 50 years. After all, even though tropical storm and hurricane warnings had always bombarded them on a weekly basis between July and November, nature had always looked kindly on this little bit of paradise. Winds reaching 60 to 70 miles per hour (96.56 to 112.65 kilometers per hour) during "the season" were not uncommon, but Grenada had somehow avoided a direct hit by anything stronger than a category 1 hurricane for almost two generations.

Then came Ivan the Terrible, a category 4 hurricane that flattened much of the island on September 7, 2004. After so many years of "much ado about nothing" storm warnings, most Grenadians were unprepared for the 160-mile-per-hour (257.5 kilometer-per-hour) winds and relentless downpour that hammered the island for hours.

The evidence of Ivan's violence is there for all to see, not only in the homes damaged beyond repair and the ravaged vegetation but also in the sad faces of the displaced, the jobless, and people

who lost loved ones. Nearly every one of the 102,000 islanders was touched by the storm, which damaged 85 percent of the buildings on the island and rendered most of its refuge sites, churches, and schools uninhabitable. Although only 39 people were killed by the hurricane itself—a relatively small number if one considers the number of people who died in the tsunami of 2005 in Southeast Asia—as many as 100 more succumbed weeks and months afterward, and the survivors are still struggling to piece together their lives.

SURVIVING HURRICANE IVAN: ONE FAMILY'S STORY

Both born and raised in Grenada, Michelle and Andrew Bierzynski share mixed lineage that probably represents just about every nationality and race of people to come to the Grenadines over the past five generations, including African, Indian, and Polish.

Today they stand on the deck of their temporary home, a duplex that they used to rent out. Higher up the hill are the ravaged remains of their former home, known as the Old Fort, where a famous Grenadian battle was fought more than 200 years ago.

"The shops were busy with people shopping for supplies on the day before Ivan struck, but most of us were still in denial. That was me, actually; I was worried about having to bring it all back to the store," says Michelle wistfully.

"There was no rain before—just a slight overcast. We were waiting for the storm, but we were mostly watching TV. Whenever a commercial came on, we turned to the weather channel. Our 12-year-old, Alena, had taken sandwiches, her hamster, and a medical kit downstairs to our basement level—partially as a game to play, I'm sure, but also because she knew that if the storm got bad, we'd need supplies. Mom was overshopping, and Dad was securing the business, so it was reasonable for the child to expect that we might miss one meal in the kitchen, eh?"

"The television began blinking," Andrew picks up where Michelle left off. "That was the first indicator, and after a while, Michelle went to check the phones and they were for naught. The rain came—typical storm stuff. I was standing in our living room near the terrace when I heard this mass of sound—not like the usual sounds of a storm but a roar. We went outside to the railing where we could see the harbor. Near the beach, the trees . . ." He breaks off, searching for words to describe the indescribable.

Michelle begins again. "Alena and I grabbed bed linens and ran into the basement bathroom. Andrew was still on the terrace, mesmerized by the sight of the storm blowing all around us. I never curse my husband, but when I looked at him standing there with this horror blowing all around us,

Michelle and Andrew Bierzynski's kitchen post-Ivan

surely about to take him away, I screamed like a drill sergeant, 'Andrew, get your ass downstairs now!'" she laughs. "He obeyed. That was three o'clock in the afternoon; we didn't come up until six o'clock the next morning."

Andrew explains, "At the fort, we have no shelter at all. We're at the top of a hill, totally exposed. Once we got the first pass, the roof peeled off. After the pressure got to be too much, I dared to begin opening and closing the door of the basement to try and relieve the pressure. The problem was opening the door; the pressure was against it, and I thought my arm would fall off. We were lucky that a piece of railing had lodged itself down the stairs and up against the doorjamb to block a lot of the major debris from getting at us.

"In a hurricane, the rain doesn't fall perpendicularly; it's horizontal. The force was 200 miles an hour (320 kilometers per hour). Our neighbors said they looked out and saw a mass of wind just crash into the fort. They saw this action and said, 'Oh, well, they're gone now.'"

Michelle nods in agreement. "We could look through the portholes of the basement and see the houses just being torn apart," she says. "The wind was so furious. I asked Andrew, 'What do you see?' and he said, 'Michelle, people are dying out there.'"

The hurricane brought furiously gyrating tornadoes, three of which hit the fort. Then in the middle of the storm came the false calm.

"At one point, it all just stopped," Andrew says. "I said to my wife, 'This is the eye,' but I needed to get out and check on my brother, who lived in the apartment attached to our garage. I went out, climbing over unbelievable debris. I had to get to him, but the mist was so thick, there was almost no visibility. I called to my brother, and after the fifth time, he answered. He had hidden under a cabinet in the apartment, which, thank goodness, proved sturdy enough.

"From 10 to 12:30 at night came more hurricane. High gusts of wind. And it rained and rained; it just wouldn't stop raining. I just kept bailing the place out. We were terrified and exhausted. And then, it all just slowed. Then it stopped."

"After the storm," Andrew says, "the walls were covered in leaves like textured wallpaper. The force of the wind was so incredible that there were leaves inside the microwave, and the microwave was closed. The same for the car, which was in the carport; bits of green were all over the inside. Bullets of wood—little fingernail-size splinterings—had penetrated the bumpers. Only an unbelievable force could drive splinters into those bumpers."

"By the morning, the mist had cleared enough so that I could see the senior citizens' home in the valley 2 miles (3.2 kilometers) below, which is where my mother lives," Andrew continues. "I could tell that it was badly damaged. I told Michelle I had to go check on my mother, and I started walking. It was light gray and very still outside; trees, of course, were across all of the roads. Debris was everywhere, and all the side roads were clogged. I got my bearings, and as I walked, I began to take it all in. Everyone I met was wide-eyed. No smiles. Some hellos, a few asking, 'How did you make out?' but because of where we're positioned on the island, most people could see by then how we'd made out."

Later, in the true aftermath of the storm, as the shock began to subside, fear, then desperation crept in.

Some people began looting. The roof had blown off the prison, leaving guards and inmates alike to seek shelter in the midst of the storm. There were reports of prisoners walking the streets post-Ivan who had not been "outside" in more than 20 years. "Many of them actually just went to check on their relatives, then went back to the prison and checked in," Andrew says.

Grand Etang Forest suffered extensive damage from Ivan

"The whole island looked like a nuclear bomb had dropped on it. The hurricane takes salt from the ocean and sprays it everywhere. And then for 3 weeks to a month after the storm, we experienced blistering hot days. There was no ice, no electricity, no running water. The hillsides were gray with salt-bake. Every tree in Grand Etang Forest is like a wooden grave marker now. Everybody got skinny; there was little food. We went on the Ivan diet. For weeks, people had that desperate look, you know?

"The residual effects of the stress became a major health factor. People were having severe problems—anxiety; the older folk kept dying. More died in the weeks after the hurricane than during it. Then, when Emily hit just 7 months later, everyone was on pins and needles. There was more stress waiting for Emily; people were so shell-shocked."

That morning, however, the full meaning of what had happened had not yet set in.

"I have a friend and business associate who is down the hill a bit," Andrew says. "He fared well, plus he had a little ice, so I had a double whiskey with him. I needed it by then. I left him after a while and continued on to my mother's.

"Eventually, as I walked, I met my oldest daughter, Nikita, and her husband. They were coming along the road in their four-wheel-drive vehicle, and she was, of course, in tears. She was the first to say, 'We're so lucky.' It was true."

HOLDING ONTO HOPE

A local man known as Spaghetti decided to ride out the storm in his newly purchased home. "Once the hurricane-force winds started to howl around me, I knew that I was in trouble," he says. "My house shook three times, was lifted off its foundation, and started to turn. I was thrown into a fig tree, and my house collapsed around me. Jumping down, I started to run for my life, and each place I raced by was destroyed behind me. The next morning, all I saw standing was a block of pillars.

Now homeless, Spaghetti is living in the basement of a benevolent friend and has been very badly affected by both the destruction of his home and the damage done to the island. "I had lived in my house for only 3 months," he explains, "and at 35, I was finally coming into my own. I'm hoping to rebuild, but I really didn't know where to turn until this wonderful family took me in as if I was one of their kids. With God on my side, I will make it through this terrible time."

CHALLENGES ALONG THE ROAD TO RECOVERY

The Grenadian Housing Authority has been completely overwhelmed with requests for help and doesn't have the resources to start rebuilding the tens of thousands of damaged and destroyed structures, especially because so many homeowners do not have property insurance.

Many Grenadians share the plight of a housekeeper named Joanne. Her home was so severely damaged that it could not be repaired. "As I don't own the land my house sits on, there has been tremendous red tape in trying to get it rebuilt; it could take several years," says Joanne. "So I have had no choice but to rent a tiny apartment for me and my son, and every time it rains, the roof leaks. It's been a tough year and a half, but you can't give up."

NEW HOPE FOR THE ISLAND

In addition to homes, schools, churches, resorts, and restaurants, the majority of the medical centers on Grenada were severely damaged just at the time when they were needed the most. Even the General Hospital lost electricity for weeks and had to rely on generated power.

"Due to the lack of power and the scarcity of fuel, we had to go back to our old ways," says Trevor Noel, assistant director of the Woodward Islands Research and Education Foundation located at St. George's University, which seeks to advance health and environmental development on the island. "We were using cast-iron pots over coal stoves instead of gas or electricity to cook with. It was back to basics by necessity for thousands of people during those critical first weeks. Staples like ice and cool water became luxuries because they were impossible to find."

After an aggressive fund-raising effort, 300 public health professionals reviewed countless houses and living conditions, and the foundation facilitated the donation of water and nonperishable goods, including pet food, from the United States and Canada. There were no serious disease or health problems after Ivan, although thousands of people were psychologically shaken and hundreds, like Spaghetti and Joanne, were displaced and did not know where their next meal was coming from.

Grenada Relief Fund

The Grenada Relief Fund (GRF) was established in the aftermath of Ivan to help individuals, businesses, and industries devastated by natural disasters rebuild and prepare for the possibility of future disasters. Primary efforts by Morgan Freeman helped the organization's first undertakings, which included building an IT training center on the island and refurbishing a majority of the island's basketball courts, which provide not only recreation but also an outlet for releasing the stress experienced by adults and children alike after the hurricane. Today, Morgan continues to support GRF programs in Grenada and beyond.

The GRF—in partnership with the United Nations Development Programme, Laureus Sports for Good, and others—provides aid for the revitalization of Grenada in three critical areas: housing, education, and industry. Between 2006 and 2009, the GRF plans to help construct hurricane-resistant homes for many of the displaced storm survivors who had no insurance and, with no alternative housing options, have been living in makeshift, galvanized lean-tos, temporary shelters, and cars.

The GRF is also partnering with various international organizations to develop and distribute superior disaster preparedness programs that will educate islanders and ultimately save lives not just in the Caribbean but throughout the world.

Last, the GRF is helping to train Grenada's unemployed for new job opportunities in industries other than farming. The IT center was its first effort; higher-education scholarships for islanders are the next step. At the time of publication, these scholarships were in development and planned for distribution beginning later in 2006.

Since its inception, the GRF has benefited from the support of many volunteers and benefactors who have given their time and talents, as well as the Hollywood arts and entertainment communities, nonprofit groups, and nongovernmental organizations. The GRF continues to seek out partnerships and information to help fulfill its mission to rebuild Grenada and make it stronger than ever. Let us know if you can help. Contact www.grfund.org for more information.

RESOURCES

ACKEE

Although it is the official national fruit of Jamaica, ackee is one of several Caribbean fruits treated as a vegetable. When cooked, ackee has the look and mild flavor of scrambled eggs. It is considered a delicacy by many and forms part of Jamaica's national dish, Ackee and Saltfish. Jamaica is the only island to consume the fruit of the tree, as it is widely believed to be poisonous if eaten before it is fully ripe. Ask for canned ackee at markets carrying Caribbean ingredients.

BANANA LEAVES

Banana leaves are used to wrap foods for steaming in Mexican, Central and South American, Caribbean, and Southeast Asian cooking. They are used only to bundle foods and are not eaten. Fresh as well as frozen banana leaves are available from Latin and Asian markets.

CANE VINEGAR

Cane vinegar is made from sugarcane syrup and has a rich, slightly sweet flavor. It is most commonly used in Philippine cooking. Higher quality cane vinegars are aged in oak barrels for a smooth taste and are used to make salads, sauces, deglazes for meats, and vinaigrettes. Cane vinegar is widely available at gourmet food stores.

GREEN SEASONING

Green seasoning is a combination of vinegar and several green herbs, such as chive, oregano, thyme, basil, parsley, and celery. It is popular throughout the Caribbean, especially in Trinidad, to marinate meat, fish, and poultry. Green seasoning is available at many supermarkets and from online retailers and should be kept refrigerated. A popular brand is Chief Green Seasoning.

PICKAPEPPA SAUCE

Pickapeppa sauce is a unique blend of tomatoes, onions, sugar, cane vinegar, mangoes, peppers, and spices created in Jamaica in 1921. Its smooth, sweet flavor provides it a versatility that has prompted the nickname "Jamaican ketchup." One of its most popular uses is to add flavor to cream cheese, but pickapeppa sauce may also be used directly out of the bottle as a steak sauce or marinade. It is available at specialty food stores as well as from online retailers.

ROTI

A staple of Indo-Caribbean fast food, roti is a griddle-baked flat bread, usually made with whole wheat flour. It is either torn apart for dipping in curries or left whole, stuffed with curried meat, seafood, or vegetables, and rolled up like a burrito. Rotis may be purchased fresh at West Indian markets and roti restaurants, many of which sell unfilled wraps by the dozen.

SAZON

Sazon is a type of seasoned salt characteristic of Latino cuisine. Ingredients vary but usually include coriander, annatto, garlic, and salt. It is used to add color and flavor to meats, fish, poultry, soups, and stews. A popular brand is Goya, which is found at many grocery stores. Sazon is also available at Latin markets as well as from online retailers.

SEASONING PEPPER

The term *seasoning pepper* refers to peppers that add flavor to a dish and encompasses a variety of peppers. Farmer's markets may sell small, flat, beret-shaped peppers marked as seasoning peppers. These peppers have the flavor of Scotch Bonnet peppers without the heat. Bell peppers are another mild substitute.

SHERRY PEPPER SAUCE

A Bermuda tradition beginning with British sailors in the 1600s, sherry pepper sauce is today found in almost every restaurant and home in Bermuda. It is made from peppers and spices steeped in dry sherry for several months, and it is known for its fiery flavor and robust aroma. The most famous brand is Outerbridges, which is widely available from online retailers.

SOURSOP PUREE

The soursop is a prickly green fruit native to the Caribbean and Central and South America. Its white pulp may be eaten raw as a dessert or used to make juice, candies, sorbets, and ice cream flavorings. Indigenous people of the regions where the plant is common use the fruit, seeds, and leaves for herbal medicinal purposes. Soursop puree is available at Latin markets.

TAMARIND

The tamarind, also known as the "Indian date," is a fruit native to Asia and northern Africa. Tamarind pulp is popular in East Indian and Middle Eastern cuisines as a souring agent, similar to lemon juice in Western cuisines. Tamarind is also an ingredient in Worcestershire sauce and in a sweet syrup used to flavor soft drinks. Jars of concentrated pulp with seeds can be found at East Indian and Asian markets.

TANNIA

Tannia is the tropical equivalent of the potato or yam in more temperate climates. It is mealy and mild like a Maine potato. Tannia may be available at Latin markets or food stores.

WAKAME SALAD

Popular in Japan and other parts of Asia, wakame is a deep green, edible seaweed treated like a vegetable in soups and simmered dishes or used in salads. Wakame salad is often wakame with only a simple rice vinegar and sugar dressing, but it may also include other vegetables. It is available in Asian markets or from fish vendors that sell sushi products.

PHOTO CREDITS

INDEX

Boldfaced page references indicate photographs.

P

Pancakes
Jessica's Tropical Pancakes with Ginger Syrup, 214–15, **215**
Pannier, Cyrille, 174–75
Black Antiguan Pineapple with Montgay Rum and Vanilla
Sauce and Soursop Sorbet, 176–77
Chilled Spiced Coconut Soup, 177
Grilled Caribbean Lobster with Passion Fruit Glaze and
Vegetable Slaw, 178
Papaya
Caneel Bay Tropical Fruit Soup, 162, **163**
Chilled Spiced Coconut Soup, 177
Grenadian Tropical Fruit and Shrimp Ceviche with Crispy
Sweet Potato Chips, 127–28, **129**
Jessica's Tropical Pancakes with Ginger Syrup, 214–15, **215**
Pawpaw Salad, 121
Spicy Papaya Relish, 143–45, **144**
Vegetable Slaw, 178
Passion fruit
Caneel Bay Tropical Fruit Soup, 162, **163**
Passion Fruit Glaze, 178
Pasta
Caribbean Blackjack Pasta, 136
Pasta au Pistou, 192, **193**
Pasta, Smoked Fish, and Cream, 191
Patterson, Garfield
Trotters Broth, 218
Peanuts
Island Crab, Mango, Ground Nuts, and Cucumber Salad, with
Mango Vinaigrette, 220, **221**
Peas
Arroz con Pollo, 20
Peppers. *See* Bell peppers; Chile peppers
Pickles
Cucumber Pickle, 234–35
Pies
Kenny Chesney's Favorite Key Lime Pie, 102
McDino's Apple Pie, 172
Raven's Creamy Sweet Potato Pie, 81
Pineapple
Banana Beignets with Pineapple Carpaccio and Vanilla Bean
Ice Cream, 124–25
Black Antiguan Pineapple with Montgay Rum and Vanilla
Sauce and Soursop Sorbet, 176–77
Caneel Bay Tropical Fruit Soup, 162, **163**
Caramelized Pineapple and White Chocolate Napoleon, 23–25, **24**
Chicken and Shrimp in a Pineapple Pontoon, 182–84, **183**
Grenadian Spice Cake with Rum-Marinated Pineapple,
132–33, **133**
Grenadian Tropical Fruit and Shrimp Ceviche with Crispy
Sweet Potato Chips, 127–28, **129**
Jessica's Tropical Pancakes with Ginger Syrup, 214–15, 215

Mango Relish, **164**, 165–66
Pineapple Tarte Tatin, 28–29
Plantains
Black Bean Soup with Tostones, 130
Caribbean Whole Red Snapper with Honey-Roasted Plantains
and Spicy Papaya Relish, 143–45, **144**
Jerk Lamb Chops with Two Kinds of Plantain, Red Beans, and
Coconut Rice, with Tamarind Glaze, 112–14, **113**
Local Chicken Soup, 89
Pork
Trotters Broth, 218
Pork sausages
Cajun Gumbo, 80
Potatoes. *See also* Sweet potatoes
Chicken Roti, 10–11
Island Potato Salad, **164**, 165–66
Jamaican Curried Tofu, 62
Jamaican Pepper Shrimp with Wasabi Mashed Potatoes and
Ackee Sauce, 50–51
Local Chicken Soup, 89
Poultry. *See* Chicken
Pudding
Antiguan Bread Pudding, 181
Baked Banana Pudding, 216, **217**
Cherry Coconut Banana Pudding, 216
Pumpkin
Chris's Ital Soup, 60–61
Purcell, Vivian
Hot Chocolate, 232

Q

Quesadillas
Conch Quesadillas, 92

R

Raisins
Antiguan Bread Pudding, 181
Picadillo, 18, **19**
Rum-Raisin Ice Cream, 55
Red Crab, The
The Red Crab Crab Backs, 222
Red snapper
Caribbean Whole Red Snapper with Honey-Roasted Plantains
and Spicy Papaya Relish, 143–45, **144**
Escovitch Fish, 201
Racecourse Fish in Rundown, 64, **65**
Snapper Roasted in Banana Leaves with Mango–Black Bean
Relish, 118, **119**
Stuffed Red Snapper, 211–12, **213**
Regent Beverly Wilshire, The, 110–11

P

Pancakes
  Jessica's Tropical Pancakes with Ginger Syrup, 214–15, **215**
Pannier, Cyrille, 174–75
  Black Antiguan Pineapple with Montgay Rum and Vanilla
    Sauce and Soursop Sorbet, 176–77
  Chilled Spiced Coconut Soup, 177
  Grilled Caribbean Lobster with Passion Fruit Glaze and
    Vegetable Slaw, 178
Papaya
  Caneel Bay Tropical Fruit Soup, 162, **163**
  Chilled Spiced Coconut Soup, 177
  Grenadian Tropical Fruit and Shrimp Ceviche with Crispy
    Sweet Potato Chips, 127–28, **129**
  Jessica's Tropical Pancakes with Ginger Syrup, 214–15, **215**
  Pawpaw Salad, 121
  Spicy Papaya Relish, 143–45, **144**
  Vegetable Slaw, 178
Passion fruit
  Caneel Bay Tropical Fruit Soup, 162, **163**
  Passion Fruit Glaze, 178
Pasta
  Caribbean Blackjack Pasta, 136
  Pasta au Pistou, 192, **193**
  Pasta, Smoked Fish, and Cream, 191
Patterson, Garfield
  Trotters Broth, 218
Peanuts
  Island Crab, Mango, Ground Nuts, and Cucumber Salad, with
    Mango Vinaigrette, 220, **221**
Peas
  Arroz con Pollo, 20
Peppers. *See* Bell peppers; Chile peppers
Pickles
  Cucumber Pickle, 234–35
Pies
  Kenny Chesney's Favorite Key Lime Pie, 102
  McDino's Apple Pie, 172
  Raven's Creamy Sweet Potato Pie, 81
Pineapple
  Banana Beignets with Pineapple Carpaccio and Vanilla Bean
    Ice Cream, 124–25
  Black Antiguan Pineapple with Montgay Rum and Vanilla
    Sauce and Soursop Sorbet, 176–77
  Caneel Bay Tropical Fruit Soup, 162, **163**
  Caramelized Pineapple and White Chocolate Napoleon, 23–25, **24**
  Chicken and Shrimp in a Pineapple Pontoon, 182–84, **183**
  Grenadian Spice Cake with Rum-Marinated Pineapple,
    132–33, **133**
  Grenadian Tropical Fruit and Shrimp Ceviche with Crispy
    Sweet Potato Chips, 127–28, **129**
  Jessica's Tropical Pancakes with Ginger Syrup, 214–15, 215

Mango Relish, **164**, 165–66
Pineapple Tarte Tatin, 28–29
Plantains
  Black Bean Soup with Tostones, 130
  Caribbean Whole Red Snapper with Honey-Roasted Plantains
    and Spicy Papaya Relish, 143–45, **144**
  Jerk Lamb Chops with Two Kinds of Plantain, Red Beans, and
    Coconut Rice, with Tamarind Glaze, 112–14, **113**
  Local Chicken Soup, 89
Pork
  Trotters Broth, 218
Pork sausages
  Cajun Gumbo, 80
Potatoes. *See also* Sweet potatoes
  Chicken Roti, 10–11
  Island Potato Salad, **164**, 165–66
  Jamaican Curried Tofu, 62
  Jamaican Pepper Shrimp with Wasabi Mashed Potatoes and
    Ackee Sauce, 50–51
  Local Chicken Soup, 89
Poultry. *See* Chicken
Pudding
  Antiguan Bread Pudding, 181
  Baked Banana Pudding, 216, **217**
  Cherry Coconut Banana Pudding, 216
Pumpkin
  Chris's Ital Soup, 60–61
Purcell, Vivian
  Hot Chocolate, 232

Q

Quesadillas
  Conch Quesadillas, 92

R

Raisins
  Antiguan Bread Pudding, 181
  Picadillo, 18, **19**
  Rum-Raisin Ice Cream, 55
Red Crab, The
  The Red Crab Crab Backs, 222
Red snapper
  Caribbean Whole Red Snapper with Honey-Roasted Plantains
    and Spicy Papaya Relish, 143–45, **144**
  Escovitch Fish, 201
  Racecourse Fish in Rundown, 64, **65**
  Snapper Roasted in Banana Leaves with Mango–Black Bean
    Relish, 118, **119**
  Stuffed Red Snapper, 211–12, **213**
Regent Beverly Wilshire, The, 110–11